THE LIFE

AND

EXPERIENCE

OF,

AND SOME TRACES OF THE LORD'S GRACIOUS DEALINGS TOWARDS

THE AUTHOR

JOHN GIBBS,

Minister of the Gospel, at the Chapel in Saint John Street, Lewes, Sussex.

Go home to thy Friends, and tell them how great things the Lord hath done for thee, and hath had compassion on thee. Mark v. 19.

Except a Corn of Wheat fall into the Ground and die, it abideth alone: but if it die, it bringeth forth much Fruit. John xii. 24.

LEWES:

PRINTED FOR THE AUTHOR, AND SOLD BY HIM AT 14, EAST STREET; AND AT THE CHAPEL IN ST. JOHN STREET; ALSO BY LOWER, BOOKSELLER, 51, HIGH STREET, LEWES; MR. J. WALMSLEY, 18, GEORGE STREET, HASTINGS; MR. REVELL, BOOKSELLER, BRIGHTON PLACE, BRIGHTON; MR. BURFIELD, HARNESS MAKER, HAILSHAM, SUSSEX; MR. A. GIBBS, NEAR THE GEORGE INN, TUNBRIDGE WELLS; AND BY MR. EEDES, NEWGATE STREET, LONDON.

Entered at Stationers' Hall.

Lewes: Printed for LOWER, Bookseller, Publisher, Stationer, &c.

PREFACE.

TO THE CONGREGATION
THAT ASSEMBLE FOR
DIVINE WORSHIP IN THE LITTLE CHAPEL, IN ST. JOHN STREET, LEWES.

Dearly beloved and longed for, my joy and the crown of my rejoicing in the Lord; may the blessing of God the Father in predestinating and choosing before time, and the blessing of God the Son, who gave his life to ransom all the elect from the sword of justice, and from going down to the pit of Hell, rest upon you. And may God the Holy Spirit who in the ancient councils of eternity, where all was settled, agreed to preserve till called, and at the appointed time, to convince all that should be born heirs of salvation, and to take of the things of the blessed meritorious life and death of the God-man Mediator of the best of all covenants, reveal, testify, and apply them. The three persons in unity, co-equal and co-eternal; the Trinity in unity, three persons but one Jehovah. "There are three that bear record in Heaven, the Father, the Word, and the Holy Ghost, and these three are one." 1 John v.—7. Luke x.—20. Job xvi. latter part of the 19. 2 Timothy ii. part of the 19. Proverbs iii. latter part of 32. and may you share in the good will of Him that dwelt in the bush, and know Him. "And this is life eternal, that they might know thee the only true God, and

A

Jesus Christ, whom thou hast sent." John xvii.—3. and as there are three that bear witness in the conscience; for, " there are three that bear witness in earth, the spirit, and the water, and the blood, and these three agree in one." 1 John v.—8. may these things be your happy lot and portion, so prays your Pastor.

My dear little Flock, whom I love in the best of all ties, it pleased the great Eternal I am to sanctify and set me apart in his purpose before time, and preserve in the Lord Jesus and call me by his grace, and reveal his dear Son in me. This proved to me the hope of future glory; before he formed me in the belly he knew me, and before he brought me forth out of the womb, he appointed and ordained me to speak in his name; and for the love that I bear towards you, I have, though in a very broken and imperfect manner, endeavoured to shew you some few traces of the sore trials and afflictions, that the Lord has brought me through; in hope that He will be pleased to bless the same to you at this time, or in some future day, when I am crumbling into dust. For though I know not what evil may be on the earth, this I know, the latter days are come, and the shades of the evening are not only stretched out, but are now over-spreading the professing horizon; so that most men are crying up the great light of the day; but what these men call light, I call darkness, as their light is only in the word of the gospel, short of the power of God to salvation, in delivering them from the guilt and power of their sins, and from every curse of a broken law. How true is what the wise man saith, " they know not the way into the City," but the blind are leading the blind, and if the Lord prevent not, doubtless they will both fall into the ditch together, as they have taken away the key of knowledge, they go not in themselves, and those that would they hinder. Therefore, my dearly beloved, be you aware of those that come in the outward garb of sheep, but inwardly are nothing more than goats.

But you may say, how may I know them? for the most part they will come as the wife of Jeroboam did, feigning themselves to be different persons; as you may see their picture in Joshua, ix.—9, to the 15. In word holding the doctrine of predestination and of redemption, by the precious blood of Christ, of justification by an imputed righteousness, and of the Spirits' preservation till called, and of being convicted of outward transgression, and led to believe on Jesus for life and salvation. All this may be held and much more by a natural faith, and with great light and zeal, with excellency of speech, with great ability in rehearsing numberless portions of the written word, with great outward appearance of sanctity, holiness, meekness, and humility; yet alas! all this show is nothing more than an empty profession without any real possession, and it may be said alas! All is borrowed, or as it is said that ten women should take hold of the skirt of him that is a Jew, only to take away their reproach; these will walk in hypocrisy, and handle the word deceitfully, not manifestly unto every man's conscience in the sight of the Lord, but will pass quickly and softly over the weightier matters of the new birth, or the *real* feeling of death, and the passing from death to the *real* feeling of life; and instead of casting up this way and shewing the many struggles between death and life, with great deliberation and nicety, keeping the way of the tree of life, and shewing the real character that has a lawful right thereto; they will endeavour to embolden and encourage those who are legally alarmed, to lay hold on the promises in their self-will; thus they heal the hurt of the daughter of Sion slightly, crying peace, peace, where the Lord has not spoken peace. But those, whom the Lord commissions and sends are compared to thrashers. "Behold, I will make thee a new sharp threshing instrument having teeth; thou shalt thresh the mountains, and beat them small, and shalt make the hills as chaff; thou shalt fan them, and the wind shall carry them away, and the whirlwind shall scatter them; and thou shalt rejoice in the Lord, and shalt glory in the Holy One of Israel," Isaiah xli. 15, 16. There is no fleshly tenderness here, but faithful dealing in manifestation of the truth to every man's conscience in the sight of the Lord.

Moreover, the Lord has compared his sent servants to a flame of fire, Heb. i. latter part of the 9. "Is not my word like as a fire? saith the Lord, and like a hammer that breaketh the rock in pieces?" Jeremiah xxiii.—29. This word will try every man's work of what sort it is. This will attend the sent servant's message; for the Lord has declared that the house of Joseph shall be as fire, and the house of Esau as stubble, Obadiah, 18 verse. And the Lord declares in Isaiah, "To the law and to the testimony; if they speak not according to this word, it is because there is no light in them," viii.—20. Now if a man speak according to this, (which he will if the Lord send him,) he will insist on the law entering and sin reviving, and the painful feelings of a sinner's death, before any true marriage can take place. For a woman that marrieth another man before her first husband is dead, committeth adultery, but after her first husband be dead, she is at liberty so to act. Rom. vii. —1, 2, 3, 4. Then to shew the nuptial day, to have and to hold for better for worse; Oh! the gladness of heart that attends this day of the Son of Man; it is said, "Abraham saw this day and was glad;" and the Church is exhorted to go forth and behold it. Songs iii.—11.

Here the bridegroom manifests this gift of himself, in paying all the brides debt's and clearing her from all demands of law and justice, and to set her free. "If the Son therefore shall make you free, ye shall be free indeed." John vii. —36. Then the admonition is, "Stand fast therefore in the liberty wherewith Christ has made us free, and be not entangled again with the yoke of bondage." Gal. v.—1. Thus he manifests his choice of her, although she is every way unworthy of so high a favour, which truly is better than life itself. "For what am I," says the Psalmist, "that thou shouldest choose me before the house of my father?" And this will be the wonder and astonishment of the soul of this hell-deserving sinner, who is raised from the dunghill to such an exalted state.

Therefore, my dearly beloved little Flock, seeing these things I admonish you in the language of Paul to the Philippians, iii. latter part of the 16, 17, 18, 19. And I warn you in the language of John, "If there come any unto you, and bring not this doctrine, receive him not into your house, neither bid him God speed; for he that biddeth him God speed is partaker of his evil deeds." 2 John, 10 and 11 verses. Now hear what our Lord saith, "If ye know these things, happy are ye if ye do them." John xiii.—17. And it is the desire of my heart that you may do as Moses did, "he chose to suffer affliction with the people of God, rather than enjoy the pleasures of sin for a season." As affliction is sure to fall to the lot of God's family, either externally or internally, for it is through much tribulation we are to enter in; and as folly is bound in the heart of every child of God, the rod is sure to be laid on our backs, for as many as he loves he chastens and rebukes. Amos iii.—2. But this is our mercy. Then says the royal Psalmist, "It is good for me that I have been afflicted;" and another says, "Wisdom shall be justified by all her children." We shall see sooner or later, that all our afflictions were sent in love and for our profit. "For though he cause grief, yet will he have compassion, according to the multitude of his mercies. For he doth not afflict willingly nor grieve the children of men." Lam iii.—32, 33. And for our comfort he has declared he will never lay on us more than he will give strength to bear, for as our day is, so shall our strength be, and that no trial is to befal us but what is common to God's family, and that the whole has been waded through by others before. 1 Peter, iv.—12. "Many are the afflictions of the righteous, but the Lord delivereth him out of them all." Psalms xxxiv.—19. And again the sweet Psalmist says, "I have been afflicted from my youth up." But here is thy mercy, all things shall work together for good. Therefore, James hath exhorted us, and his exhortation is, "Be patient therefore brethren, unto the coming of the Lord. Behold the husbandman waiteth for the precious fruit of the earth, and hath long patience for it, until he receive the early and latter rain. Be ye also patient, stablish your hearts, for the coming of the Lord draweth nigh. Take my brethren, the prophets, who have spoken in the name of the Lord, for an example of suffering affliction, and of patience. Behold, we count them happy which endure. Ye have heard of the patience of Job, and have seen the end of the Lord; that the Lord is very pitiful, and of tender mercy," James v.—7, 8, 10, 11.

Now my, beloved, I have in the following pages presented you with some small traces of my trying path, as much as a very broken memory could go back and gather up, as this was all I had to rely upon, having never kept the least particle written down at any time.

Reader, art thou one that seest how deeply thou art in debt, and the impossibility that appears of your ever obtaining forgiveness? You cannot labour under a more heavy dejection of mind than I have, so that I have chosen strangling rather than life, because my life was bitter within me, and heaviness of heart caused me to stoop. And surely it drank up the moisture of my spirit, so that I often concluded there could be no help for me, as I had the very earnest of future misery within me, and truly a fearful looking for, of fiery indignation, which is to devour the adversaries. And in those days I concluded I was an adversary, and that God was the same to me. Yet I lived to prove that God's thoughts were not as mine, for his thoughts were thoughts of love and kindness, but this was hid for a long time from me, and until it did appear, (Titus iii.—4.) I sunk in despondency and despair, as in deep waters were there was no standing. But he had appointed that I should be so dealt with; that I might be a pattern to those that should come after. 1 Tim. i.—16. "Wherefore he is able also to save them to the uttermost that come unto God by him, seeing he ever liveth to make intercession for them." Heb. vii.—25. This I consider to be coming to the uttermost precipice of extremity, or to the end of the law.

It may be that you may be very sharply tried in providence; this is not singular, I have been so sharply tried before you, as to have no-where to lay my head, as our Lord saith, "The Foxes have holes, and the Birds of the air have nests; but the Son of Man hath not were to lay his head." Matthew viii.—20. And I have known the time in which I have been so destitute, that had a few more days rolled over my head without supplies, I should have closed all my sorrows in this life. And many a dark cloud has passed over me, since God first shined in his providence, so dark has it been, that nothing less than a workhouse has been before my eyes, for myself and my family; with sinking in circumstances for not less than three years together, and harrassed with the thought of what I should obtain to eat and how I and mine should be clothed. But these troubles I always kept closely to myself, and never made poverty a cloke to move the compassion of any one, neither did I beg of any person, borrow of any one, nor did any one relieve me by any secret gift, but my manner was to pray to my Father in secret, to hide my sorrows from man; and my heavenly Father has rewarded me openly, and has often appeared for me; so that I can say with good old Jacob, "He has fed me all my life long and redeemed me from all evil." And I exhort you to go and do likewise.

It may be you may be tried another way, you may be cast out by man, forsaken by all your friends, and pushed hard at by your enemies, this is a trying path which I have also been in. I have in my childhood been forsaken of my parents, As "the Ostrich leaveth her eggs in the earth and warmeth them in dust, and forgetteth that the foot may crush them, or that the wild beast may break them; she is hardened against her young ones, as though they were not hers; her labour is in vain without fear; because God hath deprived her of wisdom, neither hath he imparted to her understanding." Job xxxix.—14, 15, 16, 17. So have I been left friendless in the open world, and I can say, I have seen affliction from my youth up; and as one says, " few and evil have my days been;" for if I have seen the cloud, in providence remove for a season, the clouds of adversity have soon returned again. Thus far I find changes and war abide me. I have had some close acquaintances who have stood by me, some of them from ten to fifteen years and after all these years, having so long walked together in pleasant council, they have forsaken me in the day of great trial, and instead of succouring me they have fallen upon me. " And they said unto him we are come down to bind thee that we may deliver thee into the hand of the Philistines; and Samson said unto them, swear unto me, that ye will not fall upon me yourselves." Judges xv.—12. They left me and walked no more with me. "From that time many of his Disciples went back and walked no more with him." John vi.—66. "This Moses whom they refused, saying, who made thee a Ruler and a Judge? The same did God send, to be a ruler and a deliverer by the hand of the Angel which appeared to him in the bush." Acts vii.—35. Moreover, I had some of the greatest men of our day, and some of whom, I have no doubt, were good men, these have combined in casting me out and crying me down, because I could not admit that they were infallible, but that in many things they offended and were subject to failings; they therefore never ceased pursuing me with bitter words, and all because I refused to call any man master on the earth; and instead of their holding up my head, they have all to a man cried me down, and endeavoured to push me over the brow of the hill, as they did my Lord and Master. Well may it be said "Lord, what is Man? Or the Son of Man he is not to be accounted for." I pray God that he would not lay these things to their charge, for they saw the anguish of my soul in those days, and meant it for evil, but God meant it for good. But what has been far worse for me, was, that the Lord has often seemed to leave me and care no more for me; and I have under this cried out. "He has forsaken me, my God has forgotten me, and his mercy is clean gone for ever;" and have often cried out, "All these things are against me," but I have since proved that it all has worked together for good, and I hope you will all have to say the same. Remember our Lord and Master was of no reputation, and his face was more marred than any man's; they that saw him without fled from him, but he hid not his face from shame and spitting, therefore it is said that they spat in his face and smote him with the palms of their hands. And shall the servant expect to be above his master, and if they have called the master of the house Beelzebub, what can be too bad for us? They shall speak all manner of evil of us, and hold us up in the darkest shades. It was said of our Lord, that for the glory that was set before him, he endured the cross and despised the shame; may we be armed ourselves with the same mind, and choose rather to suffer affliction with the people of God, than to enjoy the approbation of man, which at the most can be but very short indeed; men may frown on you, and God may also seem to frown in his providence, and yet you may be to him as the apple of his eye. Now I say to you as Jacob said unto Joseph, " Moreover I have given to thee one portion above thy brethren, which I took out of the hand of the Amorite, with my sword and with my bow." Genesis xlviii.—22. " Out of the eater hath come forth meat, and out of the strong hath come forth sweetness;" and may the Lord grant that you may take up the fragments, and may they prove as sweet to you as they were to me; then you will not be ashamed of the testimony of the Lord Jesus, nor of me, his very low, illiterate and despised servant, but will cast a mantle of love over all my weaknesses and many failings; and will pray for me that I may finish my course with joy, and the ministry which the Lord has given me; for had it not been for the love that I bear unto you, a little body gathered under me, such as were in debt, such as were discontented and in distress, I should never have published this little tract, but should have remained in silence. But for the love I bear unto you, I have desired and do still desire, to spend and be spent for my Lord's honour and for your sake. And as my Lord and master has declared that, "it is not by might nor by power but by his spirit," and as he giveth no account of his matters, he is able to attend it with a blessing; for all things are possible to him with whom we have to do, he hath all power in his hand, he will work and none can let or hinder.

I pray that the Lord will accept of my willing mind in serving him, although no one has greater cause, than myself to grieve and lament his insufficiency and many imperfections. I can say, if any have cause in this imperfect state to grieve, I more than all, for I feel that in and of myself, I am not sufficient to think a good thought; for without his special aid I can do nothing.

I pray you all that ye accept this small token from me in love, and may the Lord grant you the spirit of prayer, that you may pray for a blessing on it to yourselves and others in reading it; I therefore bid adieu to you at present, in the words of Jude the servant of the Lord Jesus Christ. "Now unto him that is able to keep you from falling, and to present you faultless before the presence of his glory with exceeding joy. To the only wise God our Saviour, be glory and majesty, dominion and power, both now and ever. AMEN."

Thine to serve,

JOHN GIBBS.

TO THE CARNAL PROFESSOR.

Perhaps my reader may be ready to ask who I mean by this character. My answer is, every one that stands in a profession of the Gospel, taking hold of, or claiming children's bread in the same state in which they were born, having never been *born again* of the spirit, but only convicted of their outward sins by the letter of the law, and under this conviction, holding that by the law no flesh living can be justified, they have taken hold of the promises in their own strength, and have believed with a natural faith, which hath produced a circumspection in their moral life, and this has caused them with great zeal to cry out against outward sin; and press up an external appearance of holiness; thus they say in their hearts, " Stand by thyself I am holier than thou, Isaiah LXV. —5. I am no extortioner, adulterer, nor unjust person, Luke xviii.—11. For I am growing in holiness better and better, I am so regular and strict in my duty, that I seldom or ever fail in that; but if I do, I never rest until I have by double diligence done penance and recovered myself, then I am happy again, and conclude, God is better pleased with me to day than he was yesterday, and hope I shall be more guarded in future; and if I be, I shall enjoy peace again, and God will be better pleased with me." This is the character I consider to be a carnal professor.

Now if this feeble performance should fall into thy hand,

it will be like an arrow drawn at a venture by the author, which will enter the joint of your harness; or " like a two edged sword it will be quick and powerful, descerning the thoughts and intents of the heart, piercing even to the dividing asunder of soul and spirit, and of the joints and marrow," Heb. iv.—12. For honest conscience will say, I am a stranger unto the things this author speaks of and insists on, and the natural enmity of the heart will rise up (though against conviction) and resist the power of truth.

Another witness will rise up and say, " Alas ! If this be true what will become of me, and hundreds more? And I cannot say that it is an untruth, for the author insists on the law entering which gives the knowledge of sin and brings the sinner to death ; from thence he receives faith, which is the gift of God, and by the self-same power, which brought the Lord of life and glory from the dead, this man is brought through the strait into the manifestation of life, and the enjoyment of that peace, which flows through the death of a dear redeemer." But another will arise that is at enmity against it, and begin to cry out, " he limits the holy one of Israel in bringing all one way ; what are not any drawn by love ? I will never believe it ; for my good reverend friend declares, if a man have but a desire, and calls on God and believes ; he is safe. Therefore, I will lean to what he says, for he crieth peace, peace, and so I will have it. Away with such a fellow from the earth, he is not fit to live," Acts vii.—51, 52, 53, 54. Now this I will say to such a one, " you have been warned, and if you take not the warning, I am clear from your blood." And I say again, though your confidence be ever so strong in the sound letter of the word, and though your life be like that of an angel's, it is nothing more than knowing Christ after the flesh; " Yea, though we have known Christ after the flesh, yet now henceforth know we him *so* no more." 2 Cor. v.—16. And my Lord says, that all such knowledge profiteth nothing, John vi.—63. And Paul says, " He that is in the flesh cannot please God." Rom. viii—8. Now being in the flesh, is, having all the sound word of truth in your judgment, and your outward appearance like unto a white-washed wall, or a grave turfed over; but after all never to have known what it is to be brought in guilty before God, with your mouth in the dust, if so be, there might be hope, and to accept of the punishment of your sins; being without hope, and according to your knowledge, without God in this world: and here to have the door of hope opened unto you, and to be raised by the spirit of life in Christ Jesus, and made free from the law of sin and death; also, here to receive a full remission of all your sins through the application of the precious blood of the Lord Jesus. Now whatever you may claim or pretend to, if this has never been experienced by you, all will prove at last to be null and void, and will never be confirmed by the Lord himself; however he may let this false confidence stand, it will surely give way; if not in this life, either at death or afterwards. For he will say, " I tell you, I know ye not whence ye are, depart from me, all ye workers of iniquity." Luke xiii.—27. And woe be unto you if he should say, " I also will laugh at your calamity, and mock when your fear cometh." Prov. i.—26, 27, 28. Now I know such a character will fight and rebel against the truth; but woe be to him who is found living and dying in such a battle as this, better had it been for that man, had he never been born.

TO THE LEARNED.

If any such should condescend to stoop so low, as to peruse this simple, ungarnished Narrative. Perhaps my reader may be a professed reverend divine of the High Church, if you should be one of these high dignitaries, I trust you will by comparing the matter contained in this little tract, find it not contrary or repugnant to the contents of the 9th, 10th, 11th, and 17th articles of your professed Church.

But, should a learned layman be induced to peruse it, either to make sport of the illiterateness, or the unpolished style of the uncultivated penman; I have a word to drop by the way to such. First, this little faithful Narrative was not written for any to sport with, but intended for those who are afflicted in mind, body, or circumstances; without help or succour as to this life. For the Lord has said, I will leave in the midst of thee, a poor and afflicted people. Therefore I would caution you not to be too curious, seeing what it has cost others. "He smote the men of Beth-shemesh, because they had looked into the Ark of the Lord, even he smote of the people fifty thousand and threescore and ten men; and the people lamented beause the Lord had smitten many of the people with a great slaughter." 1 Sam.vi.—19. Neither sport with things you are not acquainted with. Consider what it has cost some that made sport with one of God's family. Judges xvi.—25. you may read in the following verses what an awful end they came to. Therefore I beg of you to lay by your light sporting spirit or lay by the book.

Now a word to the more grave and learned man. Whatever may have been the secondary cause to induce you to peruse it, the Lord only knows. But should it be to see the nakedness of the outward land, or the weakness of the performance; I would advise thee two things; first, weigh well this portion of scripture, " Because the foolishness of God is wiser than men; and the weakness of God is stronger than men. For ye see your calling, brethren, how that not many wise men after the flesh, not many mighty, not many noble, *are called*. But God hath chosen the foolish things of the world to confound the wise; and God hath chosen the weak things of the world to confound the things which are mighty; and base things of the world, and things which are despised, hath God chosen, *yea,* and things which are not, to bring to nought things that are. That no flesh should glory in his presence." 1 Cor. i.—25, 26, 27, 28, 29. And the next is, to remember the Author was altogether destitute of a friend to give him the smallest degree of education. Therefore I am like an instrument in the rough, unpolished; and if you have the great advantage of learning over me, this lays you under the greatest obligation of gratitude, first to God, for giving you friends so mindful of you; and secondly, for the means of enabling them to render you so great a service. Therefore I admonish you not to look down with contempt on the man that is destitute of human learning. I would say unto you as our Lord said, " Render therefore unto Cesar the things which are Cesar's, and unto God the things that are God's." Math xxii —21.

The Life, &c.

I have often read of men being thankful for being born of professing parents, but this has been no cause of thankfulness to me; although I do consider it to be a great mercy, when the life and conduct of the parent in private, as well as in public, adorns that profession in all things; but if a parent's outward or public shew is one thing, and his private conduct is another; if he is one thing abroad and another at home; the child will not profit by that parent's profession, but quite the reverse, Solomon says that, "the Hypocrite with his mouth destroyeth his neighbour." Prov. xi.—9. Job xvii—8. How much more then his children? for a parent's conduct is watched by them much more closely than most parents are aware of; and I am persuaded that 'tis the parents' secret conduct which oftentimes prejudices the children's minds against the truth, and causes them to go into great error, and is the secondary cause of their stumbling at the truth. Oh! what a lamentable thought!

that a parent should, by his private evil, be the secondary cause of his children's perishing. It may be replied by the reader, that a sound creed held either by parent or child, without a change wrought in the heart by the Holy Ghost, is of no avail. This I firmly believe; but I would ask him this question, suppose a man whose secret conduct thus contradicted his profession was to chide and rebuke his child for folly, and insist on the necessity of the Spirit's applying the law as the plough to make known the evils of the heart, and then the great Atonement to purge the conscience, and that unless this is done, everlasting ruin must be the result; would not the child retort, and say, " Physician heal thyself, thou art not the man within that you appear without?" And if this should be the truth, what a lamentable reply it would be! I am persuaded that the advice of many a person is lost on this account.—On the other hand where the man has had the depravity of his heart discovered by the coming of the law, for by that is the knowledge of sin, and has fallen down where " there was none to help," Psa. cvii.—12, 13, and in his affliction has sought the Lord, and the Lord has stretched forth his arm, and said, "Deliver him from going down to the pit, I have found a ransom," Job xxxiii—24. The declaration of that man will be, " He, sent from above, he took me, he drew me out of many waters," Psa. xviii.—16, and a filial fear and tender conscience is always an attendant of this work; therefore his cry will be, hold me up in thy path that I may shew out of a chaste conversation, coupled with fear, that I am a follower of the despised Jesus; and although he cannot do the things that he would, by reason of the inbred corruptions of his heart, which cause him to cry and groan to be delivered from this body of sin and death; yet, where Grace is imparted, it teacheth to deny ungodliness and worldly lust, and to live soberly and righteously in this present world; and where this is the case, that parent's religion will more or less be held by his children in reverence and esteem, and his word in some measure have a place in them.

But, as I before said, I could not be thankful for having been born of a professing parent, and for this reason, because my father's moral life differed from and contradicted that which was on his tongue; and by these means, my mind very early received such a prejudice against all Dissenters, that if it had been in my power, I should have compelled all to have gone to the High Church.

But now to come to my promised subject, I have been informed that I was born and brought forth into this Vale of Tears, Job, v.—7. Ecclesiastes viii.—6. on the 20th of October, 1769, in a little village called Ditchling, about eight miles west of Lewes, and eight miles north of Brighton, Sussex. A few years before my birth what was called the Gospel was brought to Brighton, and from thence to a large house called *Oat-Hall*, in the parish of Wivelsfield, about three miles north of Ditchling, by the Countess Dowager of Huntingdon. What this woman knew for herself, I will not pretend to say; great was her zeal, and her *all* was spent on that cause; but the Apostle says, though a man may give all his goods to the poor, and his body to be burned, yet if he be destitute of charity, or the love of God, shed abroad in the heart by the Holy Ghost, all is of no avail, but he will at last be a cast away. 1 Cor. xiii.—3. Let not my reader conclude that I *condemn* that bountiful woman; I only say that the Apostle allows that all this may be done, and yet there be no deliverance from the curse of a broken law, nor from the sting of death, because every one must receive the love of God in the heart to cast out slavish fear that genders to bondage. This great woman, the Countess of Huntingdon, hired a large house, which stands at the east entrance of the village of Ditchling, to this day, she hired it for her occasional residence, as it lay conveniently between Brighton and Oat-Hall, and in her absence, her custom was, to send her spare priests to this house, to wait her orders for removal to any place she thought fit; and she engaged my Mother to keep this house, and wait on her ladyship when there, and in her ladyship's absence, to wait on these priests, and for this, she was to live in the house rent free; and my Father used occasionally to preach in the absence of these priests, at the vacant places, but my Father still followed his trade.

Now I shall bring my reader to the great loss that befel me, from the effects of which, I did not recover for many years. At the time when I was but a few months old, one of the Countesses priests had a child that failed with the small pox at Brighton, and he was therefore obliged to remove from that place, and what did he do? but come down to this house, as no one there could prevent him, the house being a receptacle for all of his class to come to, that chose so to do; but did he come as an open enemy? No, but wrapped in disguise, for when it was discovered that his child had got the small-pox, he flatly denied it, and declared it to be the measles, although it was afterwards found out that this man had caused the child to be innoculated with the small pox. What think you of such a priest as this, who could in these circumstances come to a house, where he knew there were four small children that must fall victims to having a disease, which at that time was considered almost always fatal when received in the natural way? But he not only did this, but when the family, that is to say, my Mother and all her children failed with the small pox, caught from his child, he slipped away, and never gave a single mite towards defraying the expenses, neither was he ever after heard of by any in that place or in those parts. Now who were the worst, this man, or those that hid him? Surely there was no rendering four-fold in him, nor in those who hid him. This took place in August, in very hot weather, in the midst of harvest; at a time when the summers were very hot; and at a time that all people were almost as much alarmed with the disease, as they would have been at the plague. My Mother, a worthy woman, even to admiration, as I have been informed; was hurried away with her poor children to the farthest part of a Common to a lonely house, in the care of a drunken woman, only; never to see her husband, or mother, or any other of her relations or friends more; and as she was sinking out of time, she saw one of her children depart this life, and the other three quite blind, and me at her breast. Reader, it may be that you have, at times, concluded that no one has had so much trouble as yourself; for a moment consider this woman's trouble at the close of life. How it stood between God and her own soul, I know not, as there was not any person with her but this bad woman in the character of a nurse. After a time, I, and two of my brothers surmounted the shock, well might the Apostle say, "The Lord separated me from my mother's womb, and called me by his Grace, and revealed his dear son in me." Gal. i.—15. It is clear to me that there is a set time for every purpose under the sun, and that nothing shall hinder his purposes from being accomplished. He purposed to bring me into this world, and appointed the instruments, and as soon after as my mother had fulfilled the day she was appointed for, she dropped out of time; her work was finished. My father's mother took two of the three children to bring up, not doubting but my father would bring up the little one with great tenderness; but alas! what is man? No sooner was my mother taken away, than I lost my father, that is to say, his tender, parental feelings. For he cohabited secretly with another woman, which soon drew all his love from his offspring; and as one bad step soon leads to others, so it fell out with this man; he became secretly given to drink, which caused me to go with many a hungry belly and ragged back,—so that my life has often been a burthen to me.

When I was a child, and before I can remember, I was carried to a place called Saint John's Common, and the first thing that I can remember, was, being turned out of doors in a cold day; and the next thing that having had given to me a piece of beef, I was devouring it greedily, being pinched with hunger, when it almost finished my race, for it hung in my throat and a bystander seeing me almost gone, caught, and held me up by the heels. These means were blessed, and it came back again. O! that word "preserved to a future day of call." How clear this has appeared to me at times! The next danger that befel me, was, being pursued—not less than a mile on the open Common, by a furious bull, when I was about five years old; but when my little heart was near bursting, unexpectedly a dog crossed that way and sprang at the bull, which drew his attention from me, or I must have fallen a victim to him, as there were none near to rescue me. Soon after this, I was carried away to a place called Bolney, at this place I abode a few years. Here I met with some dangers, but far greater sufferings; for as I grew older my nature required more nourishment, and as hunger is keen in growing children, so I felt it. I have often envied those that had a mother, knowing that 'tis very rare any change ever damps her parental care and love to her offspring; but how often has it been seen and felt, that after the death of a loving mother, the father's affection hath died away, and he has become like the Ostrich which leaveth her eggs in the earth, and forgetteth that the foot may crush them, or that the wild beast may break them. Job xxxix.—14, 15. Of several dangers that I met with in this place, one that I never shall forget was, I got up into a lofty tree and my foot slipping, I fell, and if I had fallen to the bottom, in all probability, I should never have rose again in this life. But Oh! the preservation of me, even in those days; it was preordained, that there should be the heart of a decayed limb, which abode firm, on which I fell, and that part held me, and with great difficulty I extricated myself; even at that time I was lost with wonder and amazement that I did not pass that limb, as I fell with such great force. Another narrow escape I had, was, as I was helping a man loading of bark, in the hope of having a ride on the waggon. This man being careless of the consequences, let me ride on the top of the bark, not warning me of my danger. But Oh! when come near the barn's door I saw my danger, but Oh! too late. I cried out, but no man regarded me, I saw that I must fall, or else be crushed against the beam over the entrance; and, the horses, as they commonly do at such places, began to plunge; there was no time for me to parley, venture I must, or fall from the top of the load. In my haste, I chose the former, but O when the waggon came in contact with the barn's floor, I felt as though my breath would be pressed out of my body, and a very narrow escape it was, the beam tore the skin off my back, and made me sick and faint.

Another narrow escape that I had, was, as I was roaming one day, I found, as I thought, a great prize:—namely, a Woodpecker's nest in the hole of a beech tree, with great eagerness I ascended the tree, and with some difficulty worked my hand into the hole, not considering that it would be more difficult to draw my hand back again. But I soon found that I was become a prisoner to the tree, and would have been glad to have left the prize, although the nest was full of eggs; but I could neither take the prize nor leave it. Oh! how did I endeavour to draw my hand back, but the pain it occasioned caused it to swell, and many tears I shod in that place, it being a desolate place where I might have perished and no man have known it, as there was no path near it. But at length, after many cries and tears, I was released. Several more dangers and as great, I could mention, but lest I should tire my reader, I forbear. I wandered about this place, I suppose about four or five years, at times in cold, in hunger, and almost in nakedness; and as one part of my employ was to fetch gin for my father, I have often gone to a house for this destructive drink, and there have seen the table well spread for the children, the smell whereof has made me sick, I being so empty, and I have shed many a tear on returning, and vowed that if I should ever live to become a man, I never would be drunken; and drinking has never been any temptation to me. In all this trying state that I was in, I often looked at my father, but said nothing, seeing his mouth so full of what is generally called religion or gospel; for, of the talking part he had enough for a whole village; but the doing part was wanting, it rested wholly in his head; his heart never having been circumcised, there being no cutting off, no cutting out, no dying to all in self, nor dying to this world. Seeing this, caused such a prejudice in my mind against all Dissenters that I could not endure them ; about this time I had many thoughts about running away, but I was as the Lepers, **2 Kings vii.—4.** To abide where I was, there was nothing but suffering ; to go elsewhere there was no likelihood of living ; I therefore did not know what to do, but I kept my thoughts to myself. At last I came to a determination to abide there no longer, and to the best of my recollection, I at that time was between ten and eleven years old, and I never afterwards received any help from my father, neither did he seek after me, nor enquire for me. My Reader, if thou art blessed with tender parents, how thankful ought you to be, and how ought you to honour such parents, especially your mother, who has such bowels of kindness. I had rather my children should treat me ill, than that they should shew the least coldness towards their mother. But to return to my Narrative, I started without one penny in my pocket, and for all the clothes that I had on my back, if they might be called clothes, you would not have given one shilling ; and as Abraham went out not knowing whither he went, so did I. I felt my mind impressed to call on a relation that lived about eight miles off, to enquire whether she knew of any place of servitude vacant, and to my great surprise, as soon as I asked her, she informed me that a lad had run away from a small gentleman's house that morning, and, what is also surprising, it was the very house in which I was born; she kindly offered to go with me to offer my services, this I gladly accepted, and we set off, and quickly had an interview with the master and mistress of the house. Oh! how my heart throbbed, and my breath became short for fear that they would despise my ragged appearance, and no less than three daughters with the two old people came down into the kitchen to look at me. I have often thought of David's ruddy countenance in the day that Samuel came to his father's house, and how the prophet looked on his brethren with approbation, but the Lord seeth not as man seeth, it is not him that approveth himself but whom the Lord approveth, and what shall be done to the man whom the Lord delighteth to honour; and it is said that the Lord gave Joseph favour in the eyes of the Egyptian.—Now the trial commenced, and the servants of Benhadad did not listen with more anxiety than I did; some said, I was much too small, others, that I was altogether unacquainted with the business, and was by no means a proper lad for them; but at last one of the daughters spoke for me and said, " he looks like a healthy lad, and his smallness is not much denial, if he will but be willing, and he will grow bigger; and I will engage to shew him any thing in his business myself, and give him some fresh clothes for I like the looks of him." This was the deciding voice, and no one replied against it, and all the important business being thus settled, I entered my new lodging for service that night; and I have reason to bless the Lord for that friend who thus spoke for me, to this day; for I am persuaded that the Lord put it in her heart, and none else, as every thing appeared to be against me. But the hearts of the children of men are in his hand, and He turneth them whithersoever he will. This I have often seen since, but Oh! the joy that attended this providence lasted long, and I never thought that I had done enough for my masters and mistresses, of whom I had six that had a command over me. I found that my new service was like what the Church of England calls perfect freedom, from the gratitude I felt for their kindness; it was something like Jacob's service for Rachel. But my new living not being like such as I had been accustomed to, a belly-full made me at the first, quite unwell; and not knowing at that time the cause, fears arose in me, that I should not be able to stop in my place; but I soon got over this; and all that was promised me by my young mistress was performed both in clothes and teaching. She is the only one of the family now living, and I have often thought that if one person excelled another in virtue, this was the one; she moreover gave me a new prayer book, and some other books. And for the first time, I began to learn to spell and read and write, as I had never had any instruction before on these subject; but truly was in every sense of the word, like a wild ass's colt.

I would give this word of advice to my young reader; never to look down with contempt on a poor ragged boy or girl; for what have you got that was not given to you by a tender parent? And if others have been forsaken of such a tender care, you cannot tell what the Lord will do for them. When my Mother was gone, and my Father forsook me, the Lord took me up; and what shall be done to the man whom the Lord delighteth to honour? I think that the last per- person to be proud is he, that has had so much spent on his education: for what might some of this class have been if, like some of us, they had never been taught even the alphabet?

But my reader may begin to wish to know what thoughts I had of religion. These I will now relate; seeing the moral conduct and the kindness of this woman (who was a member of the Church of England) so far exceeded that of my father's; I concluded that the High Church of England must be right, and that all Dis- senters must be wrong; therefore I became full of zeal to the form: yet the real sentiments of the members of the High Church I could not perfectly understand, for they preached nothing but Virtue, Good Works, and Charity: and I often wondered what would become of the poor who had nothing to give. But at times this did not trouble me, for I had a sentiment of my own; a sentiment that, until within the last seven years, I never knew had existed any where else; for I told it to no one; and yet it troubled me much; for I believed that there was no new race of mankind, but that the old race dropped out of time, and like the revolving part of a wheel, they appeared again in their turn. What made this the more painful to me was, that after I had dragged through a miserable existence in this world; in a few years I should have to appear again in the same miserable condition as I had been in before: and to face the like hardships again I thought would be doubly dreadful. Who would wonder that so many errors are broached, seeing that so great an error sprung up in my heart? But providence so ordered it, that on a certain day I was sent about eight miles, I say that providence so ordered it, most commonly I was ordered to ride, but on that day I was directed to walk; and after I had ascended the hill, a few miles, there came over such thick a fog that I lost myself, and wandered about a long time; and the weather being very cold, I had many dreadful fears that I should perish on the hill. Before this time I had had many doubts whether there was any God, or no; and could not settle my mind on this subject; neither could I ask any about it. But after I had wandered on the hill a long time, and become extremely faint and weary, I came to the conclusion, to pray that I might find my way, and that if I found my way I would for ever believe and acknowledge that there was a God who heard and answered prayer, and was Omnipresent and Omniscient, and that if I did not easily find it, I never would be afraid of futurity: for at that time I had many dreadful fears about death and a future state. Then was the first time that I prayed without book, and never shall I forget in what manner I addressed Heaven. It was after this manner, "O God, if thou art in Existence in the "Heavens, dissolve this doubt by delivering me, "and answer me quickly; and if I have no "answer, I shall take it for granted, that there "is no God, for I long to have this doubt dis- "solved." No sooner did I arise off my knees from the wet earth, than all on a sudden, a breeze of wind, and only one, came, and cleared the fog, I should suppose the space of five rods, and there appeared an object in view; and as I drew near it, I found it to be a waggon; and although I had traced the ground over and over before, yet my eyes were withholden from seeing it, until this took place. No sooner did I read on it the name, "Richard Hamshar," than I knew where I was. Oh! who is able to describe the mixture I felt of gratitude, dread, and sense of my guilt as a sinner. I never fully got over this; and when I have been going to do evil at any time, Oh! what convictions would seize my conscience; and my Vow, that I would ever believe that there was a God who sees and knows every thing we do, followed me: and sorry enough I often was, that this doubt was dissolved. From that time the fear of death and of judgment used to trouble me; yet so dark was the village where I dwelt, that I declare I never heard any one say any thing concerning these things: and I do believe that scarce any place in Britain could be more blind; it was like Jericho, "the place was pleasant," but (in a spiritual sense) "barren and the waters naught." From that time, when in trouble, I used to pray as well as I could extempore, as no written prayers would suit me; and I have often fretted that I could get no fresh ones; and no preaching that I could hear would suit me. O! how I used to admire the Gown, the Surplice, and the Band; and was bewitched by them; although I had the best opportunity of judging of the lives of the priests of the High Church, of any, as I was constantly waiting on them, and the house where I lived being their rendezvous constantly; and I do declare that their lives were far worse than many of their hearers, and especially than the family I then lived in: yet, notwithstanding all this, when they had got their gowns on, I concluded that they must be holy. By this I know that all priests' attire came from the Whore of Babylon, the Church of Rome, and she received it from the Devil, the deceiver of this World. Our Lord forbids that any man should wear a rough garment. This I am persuaded, means the gowns and black garments worn by priests. Then, I ask, where they find their precedent? Their professed Master, we find, had but one vesture, which was woven like a stocking; and the Apostle had nothing but a fisher's coat. I should like to see these men shew the command or a precedent for these things in the New Testament: I should not have meddled with this, were it not for three things; the first, having been so ensnared by this, that I thought it made the man holy; and although in truth it does not, and many go swelling about in this garb, it is all the holiness they have, and it is their aim to appear holy to deceive others, never having received the spirit of love, and of a sound mind. As no man can love the true God, except he receive the forgiveness of his sins; "Her sins, which are many, are forgiven, for she loved much: but to whom little is forgiven, the same loveth little." But there is an idol drawn in the imagination of the mind, and not the true God; who is known by the power with which he manifests himself; ' I will manifest myself unto him, as I do not unto the world.' He manifests himself to the world by creation, by his providence, by the written word, and by the teaching of men; but if they have no better knowledge or manifestation than this, Alas! their end will be dreadful.

The second is, because so many upstart novices strut about in this garb, whose pride compasseth them about like a chain. He that is a priest of the Lord should be the last man to be proud, for he is servant of all.

And the third is; having been smitten by so many, because I have not put on a black coat. I profess to be a Protestant; that is (if I understand the meaning of the word) one that protests against the Whore of Babylon altogether, body spiritual, and rags: I have no objection to black, so far as it respects the colour of the cloth as used in common, and not for the purpose of appearing particular; let it be so worn and it looks comely: but if a man change his habit because he is become a preacher, it shews to me that that man is not purged from the Whore of Babylon.

But to return; my mind was greatly concerned, and my inquiry was, "How shall mortal man be just with God?" Job ix.—2. And "What must I do to be saved." Acts xvi,—30. But I kept this close to myself; and as I had a great opportunity of hearing many different priests, I still had an hope, that one day I should have my inquiries satisfied; but was constantly disappointed. After I was free from service, I have often gone four, five, or six miles to hear a fresh priest; but to no purpose; of the sermons of some, I could understand scarcely a word, in consequence of their high language, or bad delivery: so that at last I was quite worn out, as I could hear nothing, but of Virtue and Works.

In this same family I lived above five years; and I bless God that gave me favour in their sight. While I lived there, several dangers befel me, which nearly cost me my life. Once I fell from a large hay-rick, one windy day, with an hay-cutter in my hand which entered my knee, and I have the mark of it to this day. A short time before, in the parish of Lindfield, a man fell in like manner, and the hay-cutter entered his bowels, and he dropped never to rise more. What a mercy that it was not my lot! If it had been, I should have lifted up my eyes in Hell. Another narrow escape I had, was thus; I had cut the ice day after day, in a deep pond, for the cows; one night there came a great snow, and like a careless lad, fearless of danger, I was going to remove the snow to cut as I had done before, when I trod on the place where the ice had before been cut, and as the snow prevented the ice from being thick it gave way, and in I slipped, and just as I sunk up to my shoulders I caught hold of a small twig of willow, not thicker than my little finger, and that was covered with snow, so that I did not see it until I felt the benefit of it; and what is surprising, this was the only one all round the pit. As the pit or pond was in the middle of the field, and as no person was eye witness of my peril, none could have holpen me; but Oh! how safe I was, although I knew it not! Even at that time was I bound up in the bundle of eternal life.

My day was short before trouble came; my master died. Then another remove must be made by me, but where to I knew not; this was like turning out of a warm bed in the cold night. But the purposes of the Lord shall stand, and he will do all his pleasure, Isaiah xlvi.—10, and the bounds of our habitation were fixed, before we were born, Acts xvii.—26. Now then for a new place; one church priest above the rest took a great liking to me, and said that he would take any trouble for me; and he thought that he had got a good place for me; but Oh! how this kind friend was deceived! When the time came for me to go to this new place, this kind friend lent me two horses, one for me to ride on; and the other for his lad to carry my little All. Oh! how my heart was lifted up in this journey! But how true it is that "pride goeth before destruction, and a haughty spirit before a fall," Prov. xvi.—18, 19, and so I soon found it. The place I was going to, was about twenty miles off, and called Storrington; to the house of a Clergyman of great note, who kept four men servants, and as many maid servants. I had not entered this house long, before I was shocked at the conduct of these servants, for they lived in all manner of debauchery, too filthy to mention. I have heard it said, that a man-of-war is nearest like hell of any place;

but surely it cannot be worse than this house was. But if you ask me which were the worst; the men or the maids? I think the latter; I was so shocked at them, that I did not know what to do; and being of a sober turn of mind, and having such a fear of death and of judgment to come, I dared not to do like them; but I found Solomon's words true, that " a Whore is a deep ditch," Prov. xxiii.—27, and that "Childhood and Youth are vanity. Eccles. xi.—10. I being but about seventeen years of age, I was in a great strait; for if I abode here, I was certain that I should fall in this snare; and how to get away I knew not. I pity the youth that meets with an inticing woman; and suppose that he should meet with three or four as I did, and yet escape; What a wonder? I thought I would apply to my master to let me go away, which I did; he asked me the reason why I wanted to go; but I was too shy to tell any one; he therefore refused me my request, alledging, that he would rather part with any one of his servants than me. I afterwards made the second, and the third request to the same effect; but he at last told me, that if I did not stay with him, he, being a magistrate, would have me confined in a prison. Now thought I, if I stay here, I shall be ruined both body and soul; and if I attempt to go away, I shall expose myself to the confinement of a prison; what shall I do? At last I came to the desperate resolution of leaving without my master's knowledge or consent; therefore, I determined to leave all my work done up in perfect good order, that there might be no fault to charge me with on that head; but then a great obstacle started in the way, which was, my having paid out of my own money, nine shillings and sixpence, for my master's letters and parcels; and having so little of my own, the leaving my wages and money paid, behind me, was grievous; but, thought I, leave you all I must; if not, Hell will be my portion. And I can truly say, that although hard to escape, like Joseph with his mistress; I left them undefiled. This was the Lord's doing, and 'tis marvellous in my eyes to this day. Therefore I exhort you not to compel your children to abide in a place to which they have a great objection, perhaps they may be like me, who could not tell the reason, why I disliked my place, for many years, to any person. Having come to this resolution of leaving, I arose early in the morning, at break of day, and held a parly in my own mind, which way to go; as there appeared no way but that poverty and shame must be my lot, and as the time was short, what I did, must be done quickly. This thought sprang up in my mind; I will go to my grandmother, and ask her to shew kindness to me as she has done to my brothers. Now my pride came low; I had no horse to ride on, nor servant to attend me; but took my little all on my back, and set out for a twenty mile journey on foot; and could truly say, that like Abraham, I went out not knowing whither I went. Many a tear rolled down my cheek that day, that is not forgotten to this; and many prayers, and many vows I made to the Lord, that if he would give me bread to eat, and raiment to put on, then should he be my God, Gen. xxviii.—20, 21. After many a weary step that day, in which I spent but one penny, I arrived at my Grandmother's house; but Oh my heart! how full it was when she shewed great coldness towards me; blamed me for leaving my situation; and protested, that, as she had done so much for my two brothers, she would do nothing for me; although she had considerable money at that time.

I had for a long time prayed to the Lord, to give me some trade; but all was dark in my path, and the Lord knoweth that I lie not, when I tell you, that I have envied every parish boy, nay, the very tramps, and secretly wished that they would invite me to cast in my lot with them. Upon meeting with this cold reception from my Grandmother, I thought that I had better go to my friend that got me the place, and endeavour to keep him my friend, least a warrant should be sent to fetch me back again; this was a good thought, and although I could not tell him the cause of my dislike to the place, yet, what is not the Lord able to do? This man declared that he was fully persuaded that the place was in fault, and not me; he having so high an opinion of me; and that he would stop all my fears of a prison; and would write to the gentleman and take the blame on himself. If you have kinds friends or parents who provide for you, these are nothing but foolish tales to you; but remember what a debt of gratitude you owe to them, and how you ought to honour them, and if you do not, you are the basest of mortals. I have seen many such youth paid home for their ingratitude. My old friend acquainted a Doctor of Divinity of me, and gave me an undeniable character to him. This man took the pains to ride eight miles to agree with me, and made me great offers, but I would not agree with him; he pressed me to tell him why I would not; at last I told him that I never wanted better offers, but I could not bear the thought of being a gentleman's servant, because I had so often seen, when they had been married what a miserable state many of their families had been in. This man was satisfied with my reasons, and left me.

After these tossings, the heart of my Grandmother relented; and on her death-bed she sent for me, and gave me twelve guineas, and bade me adieu, with tears flowing from her eyes. Now thought I, troubles are all ended, but alas how I was mistaken! For upon this I applied to a Shoemaker to teach me his trade, for which I agreed to give him six guineas; and all things being agreed on, I paid him the money; but in about three months, he had borrowed the remaining six guineas, so I lost all my money; and what was worse, this man being a single man, became so drunken, that I have known him not do any work for a month together; and for provision he cared not, if he could get drink, so there was no learning for me, neither any thing to eat; and many times have I cried myself to sleep for hunger, when I was about eighteen years of age. But I could not tell any one of my need, but kept it close; and I am of the same mind to this day, neither can my friends say that I am in the habit of burthening them with my troubles, and I hope that I never shall; I am persuaded 'tis far better to ask my heavenly father in secret, and he has often rewarded me openly. Matt. vi.—6. In these straits I often prayed to the Lord, and found that, as a God of providence, he honoured those cries. One time when I was greatly pinched with hunger, and knowing where some neighbours kept their victuals, I entered the place, and found a thick piece of pork; I took a slice and a piece of bread, I think that this was the sweetest meal I ever eat. I much wished to have another slice, but I durst not take any more, nor ever after, having somewhat a tender conscience, Job xxiii.—15, 16. and the fear of punishment in another world was greatly on me; I am indifferent about who may scoff, jeer, or ridicule, for I have suffered for this; my gracious Lord has arraigned me at his bar, brought me in guilty, and when I had nothing to pay, frankly forgiven me all my debts. At another time I think I should have perished if the Lord had not wrought a miracle to feed me; strange to tell, but no stranger than true. In the greatest of need, I found a piece of bacon, of not less than twelve pounds weight, (Matt, xvii.—27. John xxi.—9.) and never found any owner of it; Oh! what gratitude sprung up in my heart for so great a mercy; this I eat sparingly until the Lord sent rain on the earth. If the Lord could and did prepare a fish to preserve the life of Jonah, (Jonah i.—17.) he is the same yesterday, and to day, and will be for ever. This he shewed me in this providence; and I believe that he prepared and appointed this means to save my life, as much as he prepared the fish to preserve Jonah's Life. The Lord sent the ravens, night and morning, to the prophet with bread and flesh, 1 Kings xvii.—6, and the Lord sent me this flesh, as much as ever he sent flesh to the prophet. In that day I often asked the Lord to incline a certain tradesman to employ me; yet I was abased at the thought, being so bad a proficient; but in time, astonishing to tell, this very man had a misagreement with his men, and turned three of them away. When I heard of it, who can tell what I felt? No one but those who have been in the same straits. I had many fears and sinkings of heart, lest he would not employ me; but as necessity pressed so hard, there was no alternative left; go I must; O how I trembled when I came to the man; I asked him to give me employ; he answered, " if you was competent, I should be glad to do so," but not half so glad, thought I, as I should be. I told him that if he would but let me do some of the worst of his work, I should be obliged to him; but I did not tell him of my distress; and after he had sat a little while, he said, " come and I will try you." The servants of Benhadad did not catch the word more eagerly than I did; here was an answer to prayer; who dares deny it? Another difficulty now arose, I must have a few tools, and I had no money, what should I do? I thought I would go to a young woman that waited in a shop near, and ask her to lend me five shillings; I did so, and her answer was, " That I will, with all my heart." I received the money, and set off to Lewes, and bought as far as my money would go, all but one penny; this I wanted for some refreshment, as the day was very wet and cold, and I was wet through. With this penny I returned as far as the old west gate of Lewes, where I entered a shop, (I always think of it whenever I go to the same shop,) and there I parted with my last penny, for a loaf; this I had often done before; and then I returned home, and it rained all the eight miles back. In this man's employ I worked early and late, and the most that I could earn amounted to the sum of seven shillings and sixpence a week; out of which I had to pay for lodging, washing, and mending; I leave you to guess how close I must have lived, and I hope that you may have to guess only. The man behaved kindly to me for some time, but at last I offended him, not wilfully, but in this way; being a good reaper of my age, having been early brought up to it, I thought that if I went to reaping, and lived sparingly, I could save something against the winter, which I much dreaded, for fear that I should starve. I do not wonder at that dread, as it proved to be the sharpest winter that I ever saw; the frost and snow entered in the middle of November, and did not leave us until the middle of April. My reader may say what had that to do with your dread? I consider a great deal. You read that "the Stork in the Heaven knoweth her appointed times; and the Turtle and Crane and the Swallow observe the time of their coming;" Jere. viii—7. And if they know the time of their coming, surely also they know the time of their going. Should God give the fowls of the air such apprehension, and not give the same to man? Surely not. But this I can say, I dreaded the approach of that winter, and, as it proved, not without cause; therefore I engaged some reaping. A fellow-servant, who had been an old reaper, declared that he would go with me; and he being the foreman, my master was offended, but said but little. The time came, and we went; and I worked hard and fared hard, and at the close I had saved two guineas, which I vowed not to touch until winter; blessed be God for the impression; harvest being finished, the next day I returned to my former work, and nothing amiss being said by my master, I was glad; but the leaven lurked secretly in his heart, although his time to be avenged of me was not yet come; he waited till work should be dead and it would be almost impossible in the Weald to get a day's work. At the beginning of November I dreamed that my master told me that he had no more work for me: when I awoke my spirits sunk like lead in the water; this was on the Sunday night, and the next morning when I entered the shop the first sound that entered my ears, was, "John, I shall have no more work for you after this week." Now was his time to be avenged of me to the full. Masters, beware how you take an undue advantage of an affront from your servants, as they are not able to defend themselves, and there is One that will plead their cause. This man, at that time, I suppose was worth not less than six or seven hundred pounds, and had but two children, who were brought up in a respectable way; but I have lived to see all spent, and his children come to ruin, and glad to accept of a piece of bread. What a retaliation! Look at Luke vi.—38.

In this distress I tried many places for work, but to no purpose; at last I agreed with a man to work with him at grubbing during the winter, for my board, and took it kindly of that man, for thus employing of me; but this was not to be the case, the purposes of the Lord shall stand, and he will do all his pleasure. One night I dreamed that I was going to live at Firle, (a place about four miles west of Lewes) I mentioned my dream to a cousin, who replied, "I think it likely; we have an uncle and aunt there, and moreover our uncle has newly added to his business the trade of a shoemaker; " let me send a letter to them and ask the favour of employ for you?" This was agreed to, and thereupon he wrote, and an answer came inviting me over to see them. I again went out not knowing whither I went, and found one of my mother's sisters, and a most kind friend she proved to be to me, the remembrance of her is dear to me even to this day; she said to me "Come over and dwell with us, and for the love that I bear towards your late mother I will be kind to you;" and this promise she fulfilled.

Now I began to conclude that my path of affliction was come to an end; but it was not to be so: I had more bitters to drink, even in this place. Now fresh troubles arose, and they sprang from this cause: my uncle kept a foreman to do the business of shoemaking, this man was in the habit of acting towards my uncle as he ought not to have done. This I saw, but through fear, I never told of it; but the man being fearful that I had or would do so, did all that lay in his power to have me turned away; and so scheming was he, that oftentimes he would not acknowledge that there was any work to be done, and did all that he could to lose the custom to get rid of me; so that during two years, I often could not clear my board, lodging, and washing. O how this man tried me! I would gladly have worked if I could have got it to do, and there would have been plenty if this man had acted as he ought to have done. How often have I cried to the Lord to deliver me from this man; and in the Lord's time this man, all at once, took into his head to depart to his native town. How have I seen fulfilled that Scripture in Isaiah xxxvii.—29. After this man was gone, a very worthy man came in his room, who was very kind to me, and willing to shew me every part of the business; which was much for my future welfare.

Now my temporal troubles began to abate, but the care of my immortal soul pressed me sore, so that I knew not which way to turn, and caused me to bow down my head like a bulrush, and to spend my spare time in retirement. In this dejected state, a man who was a stranger to me, thus accosted me, "John, I perceive by your countenance, that you are depressed in spirit," (I was surprised at this, as I had kept all close and never shewed to any one any part of my troubles;) and he said that he had one favour to ask of me, and he would be bound that, if I complied, I should find myself better. I thought within myself, how do you know what is the matter with me, since I have never told any person? And this was his request, that I would go with him to hear (what he called) the Gospel; as for my part I could not understand him, neither knew I what he meant. He told me that he knew that the church parsons could not shew me the way to be saved, for he had proved them himself; well, thought I, there never was a greater truth than that; but is this Gospel to explain it more clear to me? He said that these people that preached the Gospel were Dissenters. This cast a great damp on my spirits, and my answer was, "they are a dangerous and awful people, I cannot think of hearing them, for such was my father, who I believed to be a very bad man; who talked so much about religion, but his practice was so bad that the Dissenters could not be right;" and his reply was, that the Church could not be right, for they could not tell the way to be saved, but these men could tell us the way to be saved. This word *saved*, was such a new and precious word to me that I was above half won over; and he promised me that if I did not approve, the first time, he would ask me to go no more; therefore I agreed to go once, thinking that I never should go again; for what to do I knew not being grieved in spirit.

When the day arrived, this man waited for me; and I accompanied him, with many fears lest that I should be deceived. We soon arrived at the Chapel in Lewes, when I was seated, I longed to see and hear the preacher; at length a grave old man appeared, and this was his text "Fear not little Flock; for it is your Father's good pleasure to give you the Kingdom." The first part of his discourse was, shewing that there were but few in comparison to the world at large, that had a desire to be saved; and the next, that those that had a desire had many fears that they should not be saved; that the Lord Jesus came into this world to save sinners, and that these were the characters he came to save (namely) those that desired, and had many fears that they should be lost; and that these were the Children of God. As this man poured forth this deceptive doctrine, I sucked it in; for I thought that no one desired to be saved more than I did; and as for fears, I had been for years depressed with them; and hearing of the way to be saved by the death of the Son of God, a thing that I never heard of before, I truly received the word with joy, like the stony-ground hearers; and I soon grew amazingly with joy, light and zeal; and as I had been a moral character from my youth, I adorned my profession in all things. I had but two things to contend with; one, was playing at cards, which I was greatly addicted to, this I gave up with some little reluctance; (that professor that has not cast away the cards, gives me no proof that he is come out of this world,) the other, was the scoffs, the jeers, and the mockings, that I met with. One wealthy man gave out in the parish, that if any person would give him information of any slip, or fault, observed in me, he would give one pound to him or her, and one pound to the ringers; but alas! before this man died he sent for me, and he was such a fright as I had never before seen, for he was so swollen that he could not lay in his bed, neither could he sit up as another man, but between the two posts of the bed, and partly stretched in a large chair; his thighs were as large as my body; and his mind was far worse than his body; and in this awful state he bid adieu to this world. Now (thought I,) would my fall be any comfort to you? But Oh! had I died in the state I was then in, I should have sunk as low as him.

For several years I stood in this apparently sound profession, that lifted me very high, and was enraptured with so much joy, that I often wished to close my mortal life; yet all this was nothing more than having the natural passions moved, all stood in word, and not in power. "The Gospel is the power of God to Salvation to every one that believeth," but that must be by a divine faith, not a human faith; in that state my zeal burnt with such a flame that I outran all my brethren, and spent my all on priests, and gathered them from all quarters, so that we had preachng almost every week; this I gloried in, and concluded that God was my God, and claimed him as such, and made my boast of the Lord Jesus, that he was made unto me righteousness and eternal life; but alas! all this boasting was vain, for he had not been revealed in me, but only in my head or judgment, the same as is the case with the greater part of the professors of our day. In that day of profession, I never heard any man preach the truth, therefore the word the priests of those days preached, could not try my work, for although I heard all of them, their preaching justified me and lifted me up in a false claim on the Lord of Life and Glory.

But God's time was now come to pull me down from my false profession, and where apparently there are no means for effecting this, the Lord can work without, this is clear to me, [see Acts ix.—3.] for I was as one born out of due time, therefore I call no man father, neither master, "for one is your Father which is in Heaven," Matt. xxiii.—9. therefore honour him.

Eliphaz said that "a thing was secretly brought to him, and his ear received a little thereof. In thoughts from the visions of the night, when deep sleep falleth on men, fear came upon him, and trembling, which made all his bones to shake. Then a spirit passed before his face, the hair of his flesh stood up; it stood still, but he could not discern the form thereof: an image was before his eyes, there was silence, and he heard a voice. Job iv.—12, 16. One night I dreamed that a glorious personage drew back the curtain, and said to me, "you are unwell, and if you die you will perish;" at this I awoke in a great fright, and drew the curtain back to see the sight, but I could not discern any thing. I endeavoured to compose myself, and to think nothing of it; but it corroded in my breast more and more; for the waters were come in unto my soul; I sunk in deep mire where there was no standing, I came into deep waters, where the floods overflowed me, Psalms lxix.—1, 2. I endeavoured to hold fast my claim on the letter of truth; and clung close to the doctrine of free Redemption by Blood: but this availed me nothing. It was decreed that I should fall, and the Lord had now wounded me. See Psalms xlv.—3, 4, 5. The law had its commission to enter, so that "Woe was me for my hurt! My wound was grievous." Jer. x.—19. Sin began to revive, and I began to feel such horrid workings in my heart that I had been a stranger to before; "What shall we say then? Is the law sin? God forbid. Nay, I had not known sin, but by the law: but sin, taking occasion by the commandment, wrought in me all manner of concupiscence. For without the law sin was dead. For I was alive without the law once: but when the commandment came, sin revived, and I died." Rom. vii.—7, 9. "My bruise was incurable, and my wound was grievous. There was none to plead my cause, that I might be bound up: I had no healing medicines, for he had wounded me with the wound of an enemy, with the chastisement of a cruel one, for the multitude of mine iniquities;" Jer. xxx.—12, 13, 14, I had before looked at the moral outward conduct, and if there was no flaw in that; and if there were fervent desires; I concluded that all was well: but this well set hair was become baldness, and instead of a sweet smell there was a stink. Isa. iii.—24. "For by the law is the knowledge of sin." Rom. iii.—20. The Apostle says that "touching the righteousness which is in the law, he was blameless." Philippians iii.—6. There was nothing in his moral conduct, that any could blame: but the law entered, and then sin revived. David says, "Behold thou desirest truth in the inward parts" Psa. li.—6. And the Lord says that the imaginations of the thoughts of man's heart is only evil, and that continually. Gen. vi.—5. I found that it was easy to abstain from outward sin; but I could not cease from the motions of evil within. O the filthy obscene thoughts, and workings of concupiscence that were within me! I could not cease from sin: neither could I do good. I found that I was under the curse, and my life hung in doubt. Deut. xxviii.—66. I said in the morning, would God it were even! And at even, would God it were morning!

The Lord woundeth all that he healeth; "For he maketh sore, and bindeth up: he woundeth, and his hands make whole." Job v.—18. 'They that be whole need not a physician, but they that are sick; for he came not to call the righteous, but sinners to repentance.' Matt. ix. —12, 13. And Mr. Hart says,

" Tho' all are sinners in God's sight,
There are but few so in their own."

And again,

" A sinner is a sacred thing;
The Holy Ghost has made him so."

That is, he applies the law; and by the law is the knowledge of sin. "I kill" says the Lord, " and I make alive." Deut. xxxii.—39. First, he kills to all hope and help, and then he gives life and peace. "The Lord hath chastened me sore: but he hath not given me over unto death." Psa. cxviii.—18. And the Church cries out, " Thou hast wounded me with the wound of an enemy, and the wound of a cruel one." A death blow is struck into every enjoyment in this life; for " the earth that is under thee shall be iron;" God's wrath being revealed in a fiery law; "and thy heaven that is over thy head shall be brass." No prayer being answered. Deut. xxviii.—23.

"All shall be taught of me" says the Lord. And our Lord Jesus says that, "every man that hath heard, and learned of the Father, cometh unto him." John vi.—45. And David says, "Blessed is the man whom thou chastenest, O Lord, and teachest him out of thy law: that thou mayest give him rest from the days of adversity, until the pit be digged for the wicked." Psa. xciv.—12, 14. "The law was given by Moses, but Grace and Truth came by Jesus Christ." John i.—17. Had they believed Moses, they would have believed Christ. John v.—46. "The law was our schoolmaster unto Christ, that we might be justified by faith. But after that faith is come, we are no longer under a schoolmaster." Gal. iii.—24, 25, And all that have not been under this schoolmaster, their knowledge is empty and light; and they have not inherited substance. For the Apostle says that before faith came, we were kept under the law, shut up unto the faith which should afterwards be revealed; and by faith we enter into rest, and cease from our own works, as God did from his. Heb. iv.—10. And the Lord has commanded the house of Judah not to sow among thorns, but to plough up the fallow ground of the heart. Jer. iv.—3. And where the plough has not entered, the desperation of the heart is unknown, and the letter of the word is received with joy; but where this plough has entered the hidden evils are discovered, and brought to the light. Before this, I vindicated and defended the doctrine of Election and Predestination, and held it as a precious doctrine: but the law entered, and stirred up that which was unknown before: "because the carnal mind is enmity against God: for it is not subject to the law of God, neither indeed can be." Rom. viii.—7. I knew not before, that there was *enmity* in my heart against the sovereignty of God, nay, against God himself, seeing "that it was not of him that willeth, nor of him that runneth," Rom. ix.—16, but depended on preappointment; and not on the good or evil of any man. " For the children being not yet born, neither having done any good or evil, that the purpose of God according to Election might stand, not of works, but of him that calleth. It was said unto her, the elder shall serve the younger. As it is written, Jacob have I loved, but Esau have I hated. What shall we say then? Is there unrighteousness with God? God forbid. For he saith to Moses, I will have mercy on whom I will have mercy, and I will have compassion on whom I will have compassion." Rom. ix.—11, 15. The law worketh up wrath; and I felt it arise in my heart against God as he held me under the sentence of condemnation, " by the offence of one judgment came upon all men to condemnation;" Rom. v.—18. and our

Lord saith, that "he that believeth not is condemned already," John iii.—18, and again, "he that believeth not the Son, shall not see life, but the wrath of God abideth on him." 36 v. This I found to be true, I could not love a holy and just God, as he kept his goodness and mercy concealed from me, and there was nothing in my view but his holiness, justice, and sovereignty, and his tremendous presence. "Justice and Judgment are the habitation of thy Throne," Psa. lxxxix.—14, and by reason of his highness, I could not endure his holding me under a sight of my original and actual sins, and himself a consuming fire; I fain would have fled out of his hand, but "he took me by my neck, and shook me to pieces." Job xvi.—12. I said, "Oh that I had wings like a Dove, for then would I fly away, and be at rest!" Psa. lv.—6. "Howl ye, for the day of the Lord is at hand, it shall come as a destruction from the Almighty. Therefore shall all hands be faint, and every man's heart shall melt, and they shall be afraid, pangs and sorrows shall take hold of them, they shall be in pain as a woman that travaileth, they shall be amazed one at another, their faces shall be as flames." Isa. xiii.—6, 8. The Lord asketh this question, "can thine heart endure, or can thine hands be strong, in the days that I shall deal with thee?" Ezek. xxii-14. And every heart shall melt, and all hands shall be feeble, and every spirit shall faint, and all knees shall be weak as water." Ezek. xxi.—7. And this question is asked, " wherefore do I see every man with his hands on his loins, as a woman in travail, and all faces turned into paleness?" The answer is, "Alas! For that day is great, so that none is like it, it is even the time of Jacob's Trouble," Jeremiah xxx.—6, 7, and truly I found there was none like it, which I shall shew hereafter.

This was sowing in sorrow indeed, and I wished that I had never been born, I envied the brute creation, knowing that they had no existence hereafter, but that I must exist to a never ending eternity. Fearfulness surprised me, for I had an earnest of damnation already, and concluded that I was appointed unto wrath, I being so full of rebellion, that I would, if I could, have dethroned the Almighty, because it was not left to the will of man, whether he would be saved or not, but depended wholly on the will of God alone, the first cause. " Oh!" (methinks I hear one say,) " it shocks me to hear it related," and well it may, and how much more if God should deal in the same manner with you, and in a measure you shall taste this cup, Matt. xx.—23. if you do not, you shall never reap in joy; remember that you have been warned, and that it shall be more tolerable for Sodom and Gomorrah, than for you, if you cast this warning behind your back, and resist the Holy Ghost as all your fathers did. Acts vii.—51, The Lord says he will, "work a work in your days, which ye shall in no wise believe though a man declare it unto you." Acts xiii.—41. Our Lord also saith that, "they could not believe;" and it is said that, "as many as were ordained to eternal life believed," Acts xiii.—48, and Saint Paul saith, that it is given unto us in the behalf of Christ, to believe on him, Phil. i.—29, and if you believe with a divine faith, with the mouth you will confess, to a deliverance from the guilt of sin, and curse of the law, and from death, Rom. x.—10, and if you should do that, you will find that suffering is enjoined to you, and you will be called a man of a narrow and bad spirit, for you *must* suffer persecution, 2 Tim. iii.—12. But you may have the letter of both law and gospel, and be held in great estimation for your piety, and your name be great; but let the law enter, and sin revive, and you die, and then be raised up, and testify of the same, and you will see what will follow; they will cast out your name as evil, they said of your Lord, " he hath a Devil, and is mad, why hear ye him?" They blamed the people most for *hearing* him, and 'tis the same cry in this day; and further, they say that they never will have any peace if they do. I think that a man had better have no peace, than have a false peace; but as it was in time past, so it is now. The prophets cry "peace, peace;" where the Lord has not spoken peace; and the people love to have it so.

In this day of my distress I wandered about like a blind man, seeking some one to lead me; but not one could I find. My reader may ask "Were there no preachers in those days?" I answer, yes, and as good as any in this day: but they knew nothing of the handwriting that was written upon the wall, any more than Belshazzar's wise men. I went all round these parts in search of a preacher that could describe my feelings; and had private intercourse with all the preachers about here: but they knew nothing of my case. Some of them strove to stay my sinking spirits; others to comfort me; others pitied me; some said that I had been guilty of some henious crime in secret; others, that I had sinned against the Holy Ghost, and that there was no forgiveness for me either in this world, or in the world to come. But all this would neither raise me to a hope, nor sink me further in despair; for I was a better believer than any of them, although I knew it not; for I believed in the Existence, Omnipresence, and Omniscience of God, that nothing was hid from him, and that he searches the innermost parts of the heart. This they did not believe; if they had, they would have trembled; and if they had trembled, they would have known me, and my case. For the Psalmist says that "Fearfulness and trembling came upon him, and horrors overwhelmed him. Psa. lv.—5. and "that the Sorrows of Death compassed him, and the pains of Hell gat hold upon him." Psa. cxvi.—3. And what are the pains of Hell? Doubtless the Wrath of God, and Despair. But they were strangers to these, and strangers to me, or they would not have said that I had sinned against the Holy Ghost, as it was impossible that I could have sinned that sin; although I was harrassed for years with the fear that I had.

Now to sin that sin, there are three things requisite; first, there must be Light; they said "this is the heir: come let us kill him, and the inheritance shall be ours." Mark xii.—7. Here was light. The second is, Malice; " Ye seek to kill me, a man that hath told you the truth." John viii.—40. What had he told them? Why, that "there were many widows in Israel in the days of Elias, when the Heaven was shut up three years and six months, when great famine was throughout all the land; but unto none of them was Elias sent, save unto Sarepta, a city of Sidon, unto a woman that was a widow." And that "many lepers were in Israel in the time of Eliseus the prophet; and none of them was cleansed, saving Naaman the Syrian." Luke iv.—25, 27. And what is speaking the truth? Why, declaring that the spirit ploughs up the heart to discover its hidden evils, and turn the man to destruction, and then applies the Great Atonement. The hearing of this, stirs up the enmity of a man's heart, and he despises and hates this work, and is malicious against it. The third is, trampling under foot the Blood of Christ; some may say " I never was guilty of that." This remains to be proved. The word, *blood,* is nothing; a man may hold that in respect, and yet despise the blood of Christ. The law shewed it forth in the paschal lamb, which was to be roasted with fire, and whose blood was to be sprinkled upon the lintel, and on the two side posts of the door. Ex. xii—23. This prefigured the Lamb of God who was to be roasted in the flame of God's wrath, and whose blood satisfied injured justice; and the application of it to a sinner's conscience. This is the language, "We have Redemption through his Blood, the forgiveness of sins;" Eph. i.—7. and wherever this blood is applied, guilt, curse, and condemnation are removed. This blood purgeth the conscience as soon as applied; " for if the blood of bulls and of goats, and the ashes of an heifer sprinkling the unclean, sanctifieth to the purifying of the flesh: how much more shall the blood of Christ, who through the eternal spirit offered himself without spot to God, purge your conscience from dead works to serve the living God?" Heb. ix.—13, 14. "The blood of Christ cleanseth us from all sin." 1 John i.—7. He that is washed is clean every whit. John xiii —10. A conscience once purged needeth no more offering for sin. " Having therefore, brethren, boldness to enter into the holiest by the blood of Jesus." Heb. x.—19. Now when any declare that they felt the virtue of this blood, as the poor woman did when she felt virtue enter into her to stop her running sore, [see Mark v.—28, 30] and that they have felt their sins forgiven, and themselves delivered from eternal death. Do not many upon hearing it, tread it under foot and speak lightly of it, and declare that if there are hungerings, and thirstings, and desires, this is a safe state? Although wisdom saith, that many shall call upon me, but I will not answer; they shall seek me early, but they shall not find me. Prov. i.--28. This is despising the blood of Christ. But this, no truly awakened sinner ever did; he sees and owns God's sovereignty, and his cry is, "if I may but touch his garment I shall be made whole." "Lord, if thou wilt, thou canst make me clean." Matt. viii.—2. And so far is he from despising the work of God's spirit, that he cries out, "blessed is the man whom thou chastenest, O Lord, and teachest him out of thy law." "Search me, O God, and know my heart; try me and know my thoughts: and see if there be any wicked way in me, and lead me in the way everlasting." And when he hears this work preached up, or described; although he fears that it is not his, being always something amiss in himself: yet he can, and will say to the preacher, from the heart, "I wish you God speed:" and instead of despising the application of the blood of Christ, he counts them the only happy people in all the earth who have felt its application; and could it be obtained for the exchange, if he had the whole world, gladly would he part with it all, for this pearl of price. "The kingdom of heaven is like unto treasure hid in a field: the which when a man hath found he hideth, and for joy thereof, goeth and selleth all that he hath, and buyeth that field. Again the kingdom of heaven is like unto a merchant man, seeking goodly pearls; who, when he hath found one pearl of great price, went and sold all that he had, and bought it." Matt. xiii—44, 46. But here was the mistake of the priests of those days: these men had themselves sinned against the Holy Ghost, and then laid it to me.

Daniel said that " his comliness was turned in him into corruption," Dan. x.—8. and so I found mine to be: I had been a great talker, and full of zeal, but now my zeal for these priests and their light food abated, and I began to look at them, at times, in their true light, and to perceive how it was with them, namely, that their God was their belly, and that they minded earthly things; Phillippians iii.—19 and instead of being so full of talk, I became as a dumb man; I found that word to be true in Jeremiah xxx.—14. " All thy lovers have forgotten thee; they seek thee not;" and in Jer. iv.—30. "Thy lovers will despise, they will seek thy life." And as my former lovers began to forsake me, I began to forsake them. The wound that I had received appeared to be cruel, for it struck death to all joy and comforts in this life, and the Heavens above were as brass that shut out my cry. My reader may say, " did you receive no comfort?" I answer, I could receive none from the preaching I heard, for the preachers dealt in husks, and, though at that time I knew it not, yet I have since seen that I wanted " clean provender, winnowed with the shovel and with the fan." Isaiah xxx. 24. But this they had not got, therefore they could not divide, neither could they give me a portion. But the first short and small ray of light that ever shone on me, for truly I sat in great darkness, nay in the very shadow of death, was, when I (as then was my custom) was wandering alone in a solitary place, I came to an old favourite spot, where there was no one near, and was lamenting my hard case, when on a sudden this part of Holy Writ came with power " if the Lord were pleased to kill us, he would not have shewed us all these things, nor would as at this time have told us such things as these." Judges xiii. the first and the last part of the 23d v. But this did not abide long, yet for the present it gave me time " to swallow down my spittle." Job. vii.—19.

In this my distress, I wandered about to all the places of hearing, but came away empty and ashamed; and for above two years was this my lot.

In these days the Lord was pleased to lay his afflicting hand on Mr. Jenkins, and empty him of all his fleshly confidence and human faith, so that he gave up preaching; and so will all others, if the Lord shews them their true state; and if he does not, they will go on in their delusion until they drop in company with the rich man in hell.

Mr. Jenkins retired down into Wales (his native country) for a time; and when he came back a friend of mine persuaded me to go to hear him; I say persuaded me, for I had before said that I never would hear him again, because he appeared to me to be so exceedingly light and trifling, even worse than his brethren, if it could be; and I had heard him in time past, till I was fearful that I should rise up in the chapel and curse him to his face for his lightness; and therefore for fear that I should do so, I ceased to hear him. The Sunday morning came, and I thought I would hear him once more, to please my friend. But O to my great surprise, he took this text "Howbeit the hair of his head began to grow again after he was shaven." Judges xvi.—22. And began to shew how God would shave or cut all the human strength, power, and might away by the law, and leave the great professor in a state of reprobation, as to his own view and feelings. This made me just ready to dance, so that I was troubled to withhold crying out "Hozanna!" aloud. Sarah said that she laughed, Gen. xxi.—6. and so did I, to think that I should have been so long looking through all the professing tribes, and after so many disappointments find that this man knew me, and could tell me where I was. How beautiful are the feet of such messengers! O what a value I set on this man! And so will you on such messengers, if you are one in distress or in debt, or discontented. 1 Sam. xx.—2. You will not suffer a small thing to cool your affections towards them; but you will " esteem them very highly in love for their work's sake," 1 Thess. v.—13. and you will be with them "in weakness, and in fear, and in much trembling," 1 Cor. ii. 3. and in secret endeavour to hold up their hands, as they stayed up the hands of Moses, lest Amalek should prevail. Exodus xvii.—12. But if you are indifferent as to who prevails 'tis clear to me where your standing is, and where you will end: bye and bye, some trifling failing will offend you, and in heart you will go over to the enemies of my Lord and master; and secretly be glad at calamity. When I came out of the chapel I avoided all company and went towards home over the hill, running, hopping, jumping, and crying; my heart being so full of joy that after so long a search I had found such a treasure; and 'tis said that " they wist not what to call it, and therefore they called it manna;" so it was with me, I scarcely knew what to say, but this I could say, that it was my meat and drink. But this joy did not release me out of prison, I still remained a prisoner, close confined in unbelief; and my joy was soon extinguished. Now great was the uproar for many miles round on account of Mr. Jenkins' preaching; many crying him down and declaring that he was mad and possessed of the devil. My zeal burnt for him and against the men who thus treated him. Nothing could disunite me from him for the truth sake; and what they called blasphemy, I called children's bread.

My reader may desire to know how I at this time went on in providence. Remember, that the bounds of our habitation are fixed, and however much we may object to move, or however we may choose, his purposes will stand and he will do all his pleasure. Now another remove must take place, sorely against my will; but the Lord always appoints means to fulfil his appointment, and the means of my removal were these: my brother's wife who lived in Lewes, being on her death-bed, a woman asked her whether she was not much concerned at leaving the little baby behind her, I was told that her answer was "No, for if its father should not take care of it, I am sure that its uncle will, I therefore am easy on the child's account." She soon afterwards departed this life, and my brother informed me that he could not afford to keep a housekeeper, and unless I would come to Lewes and take the charge of the child, he must put it out to be nursed. This brought me into a strait, I being loath in my then dejected state of mind to remove to Lewes where there were so many people, for according to my own feelings, I was more fit for a mad-house than a bustle; therefore to engage in such an undertaking appeared to be folly. But the child's situation weighed heavily on my mind, remembering what hardships I had been exposed to by the loss of my mother, therefore at length I complied, and when the time agreed on arrived, I set out to go to Lewes, with a heavy heart; and when within a mile of the town, I turned out of the road, behind a hedge, and fell down, and wept for the space of a full hour, contemplating and mourning over my afflicted lot.

One thing I have omitted, namely, that before the Lord wounded me I enjoyed a good state of health; but when his arrow pierced me, my health declined; and during five years that I lay in this state all medicine was useless; for if a man sinks in his soul he will sink in health. There are two things that I am at a loss to account for: the first is, that some pretend they are in great trouble, and yet look well, and are in good health. My trouble left a lasting impression on me, and the psalmist saith "whilst I suffer thy terrors I am distracted." And " when thou with rebukes dost correct man for iniquity thou makest his beauty to consume away like a moth." Psalms xxxix,—11. And I believe that in general the nervous system is much shaken. And the second thing is, how a man in the bitterness of death can take a wife; a pitiful remedy to extirpate the sting of death. In that day, although my heart was as the callous rock, I was thankful that I had no wife, nor one intended at that time, and as I feared that God would set me for a warning to others as he did Lot's wife, I was thankful that I should leave no one behind me to be ashamed or distressed on my account; for my life hung in doubt, and I said in the morning, would to God it was night. O! how long a day seemed to me: And at night I said, would to God it was morning, " so I was made to possess months of vanity, and wearisome nights were appointed to me. When I lay down, I said, when shall I arise, and the night be gone? And I was full of tossings to and fro unto the dawning of the day. When I said, my bed shall comfort me, my couch shall ease my complaint; then he scared me with dreams, and terrified me through visions: so that my soul chose strangling and death rather than my life," because my life was bitter within me. Job vii.—3, 4, & 13, 14. I wondered that the Lord did not cause the earth to open and swallow me up alive, as it did Corah, Dathan, and Abiram, feeling myself so great a sinner. Therefore in the morning light

I thanked him that I was out of hell. But in the latter part of these years I had one great mercy that I had not in the former part, namely, a little light by the ministry of the word by Mr. Jenkins, which described my feelings under the law. O how I valued the word in that day, for whilst I was hearing it my burthen seemed much lighter, and a little light shone on my path; and while the path was describing, I could say within myself, if this be the way, I certainly am in the way; but no sooner had Mr. Jenkins done, than I lost all, and the same gloom and horror seized me again. I concluded at times that I must be like Saul, possessed of an evil spirit, for when David played on the harp, the evil spirit departed from him. 1 Sam. xvi.—23. I compared myself to a sieve in that I could not hold or retain any thing that made for my good.

This change in my situation that I have mentioned, brought many trials with it, but these I choose to conceal, lest I should hurt the feelings of some of the present offspring whom I respect, and feel tenderness for. My way in providence was very crooked, and often hedged up, so that all things appeared to be against me, and the things that were seen often made me faint. But this I believed, although I durst not claim God as my God in his grace and favour, yet as a God of providence I viewed him to be to all mankind, that he fed and clothed the stranger,

Deut. x.—18, and "maketh the Sun to rise on the Evil and on the Good, and sendeth Rain on the Just and on the Unjust," Matt. v.—45. Gen. xxi.—17, and I do believe that all mankind have the privilege to call on God as the universal Father in providence. It is written that the young Lions, and the young Ravens too, cry to him for their food, and that he heareth them. Therefore I exhort you, whatsoever distress or trouble you may at any time be in, to cry against all discouragements, and he will honour your cry; and that you may prove this to be true, is my prayer for you.

In these days of anguish, I wished that there had not been any hereafter, Heaven, Hell, or God, because I had no hope that I should see God in peace; but yet I firmly believed in the existence of all these things, which made me envy even the brute creation, and wish myself in their state, because with them there was no hereafter, but with me a dreadful certainty of a future state, and a fearful looking for of Judgment. The Lord "brought down my heart by hard labour, and I fell down were there was none to help," Psa. cvii.—12, and had not the unseen hand of the Lord been underneath me, I must have sunk to rise no more. Here " every mouth will be stopped, and all the world become guilty before God." Rom. iii.—19. That he may be justified when he speaketh, and be clear when he judgeth, Psa. li.—4. This I found to be the last lesson out of the law, and the Apostle speaks of coming to the end of the law. Rom. x.—4, or in other words to receive the last lessons from it. Before this I had been like a wild Bull in a Net, Isaiah li.—20, and had rebelled against a sovereign God, who maketh one vessel to wrath, and another to be filled full of mercy, and hath mercy on whom he will have mercy, and whom he will he hardeneth, and who art thou that repliest against him. Rom. ix.—18; 20. I had replied against him because it appeared that I was a vessel already begun to be filled with wrath, for the law worketh wrath, and this is what the Apostle means when he says, " when the commandment came, sin revived, and I died," Rom.—vii. 9, and he afterwards declares that God had slain the enmity, Ephesians ii.—16, from which 'tis plain that his enmity had been alive, and had stood up against the Sovereignity of God; if not, there could not have been any need of a slaying work, and that too by God himself; again, the carnal mind is said to be enmity against God, which is a seed that we all have received from our first parents, and this is what the prophet Jeremiah [xvii.—9.] means by the heart being desperately wicked; and if you are a stranger to this, I say of it to you, as Mr. Hart says of pride;

" Tis hurtful when perceiv'd,
When not perceiv'd 'tis worse."

God is determined to slay this, and to bring us to the same place that the servants of Benhadad were brought to, with ropes upon their heads, 1 Kings xx.—32, to acknowledge our just deservings, and like the thief on the cross, to confess that we suffer justly, and receive the due reward of our deeds. Luke xxiii.—41. This is submitting, and I say that every man shall be brought to submit to God's sovereign will, before he ever has a manifestation of his goodness: first severity, then submission, then goodness revealed. He that has not come in this way, has come in at the south gate, and shall go out at the north gate. Ezek. xlvi.—9. Here the Lord brought me before I had the least knowledge of his love or kindness; but the inquiry of a rebel will be, "Is the man *willing* to be damned?" This shews to me that you are a stranger to this work. Is there no difference between a man being willing to be damned, and his laying at the sovereign pleasure of God under a view of his just deservings saying, as David did "let my sentence come forth from thy presence" Psa. xvii.—2. and as the man said "Lord if thou canst do any thing, have compassion on us and help us?" Mark ix.—22. I knew that the Lord would not help me, except he had included me in his covenant; and I knew that that was a secret that neither man nor devil knew; and therefore I often sighed like a man confined in a condemned cell. But the enemies of God's truth make a great outcry, and say, "Then we are to go to hell and not pray." Who has taught any thing like that? Surely I have not? The Lord says "in their affliction they will seek me early." Hosea v.—15, And if this is not affliction, I know not what is; "Shall I bring to the birth and not cause to bring forth? saith the Lord; shall I cause to bring forth, and shut the womb?" Isa. lxvi.--9. All this time the Lord was bringing me to the birth. But you may say "Are we all to be so long in the birth as you was, and feel the pangs so sharply?" I have not said any such thing. Consider what the Lord was fitting me for; all are not to be ministers of his word. But whoever is sent of God to be a minister shall come as deep as I did; if not he is sent of man and not of God; and you will remember when time is no more that you have been told this. An hearer's work may be short, but whether short or long, all must drink of the same cup, and be baptized with the same baptism. Matt. xx.--23. and all must come to die, or there cannot be a rising from the dead; for if we die with him we shall live with him; and "if we have been planted together in the likeness of his death, we shall be also in the likeness of his Resurrection." Rom. vi.--5. and there must be a rising to a newness of life, and if like Job, thou art brought to know that he will bring thee to death; and if the Lord weakeneth thy strength by the way and shorteneth thy day; Psa. cii.—23. thou wilt find, however short the work may be, that there is no sipping, but real drinking of the same cup that the Lord of life and glory drank of. It is said that he was in an agony, and therefore prayed more earnestly, Luke xxii-44. "and was heard in that he feared," Heb. v.—7. and " whom he did foreknow; he also did predestinate to be conformed to the image of his son" Rom. viii—29. and all shall have fellowship of his sufferings: and so it will be with you; and so it was with me, many a sharp pain attended my being brought to the birth.

Now I advise my enemies to look close after me, and I promise them that here shall be no craft nor slight-of-hand, but the truth deliberately set forth and nothing but the truth, and as our Lord said on another occasion, go and tell that fox that I work to day, and to morrow, and the third day I shall be perfected. Now arrives the decreed moment and the decreed spot, never to be forgotten. "To every purpose there is a time, and judgment therefore the misery of man is great upon him." Eccles. viii.—6. There is a time, yea a set time to favour Zion. Psa. cii.—13. This time now arrived, and the last pain or throe, previous thereto was anguish indeed. John xvi.—21. The psalmist says " the sorrows of death compassed him, and the pains of hell gat hold upon him, and that he found trouble and sorrow." Psa. cxvi.—3. Our Lord speaks of "Sorrow and Anguish;" these I found indeed, "thou turnest man to destruction," Psa. xc.—3. and I sunk in all the sensible pains of hell, so that the deep appeared ready to swallow me up, and the pit to shut her mouth upon me, Psa. lxix.—15. for I felt myself going down to destruction as sensibly as any go from the presence of God when he says, depart ye cursed into everlasting burnings, and the infernal fiend cried out to me, "'tis all over with you now." When in the twinkling of an eye, as I thus sunk, this thought sprang up within me, I will cry once more, for the last time: and this was the cry, "Have Mercy." At the moment of this misery or anguish passing in me, a light opened over my head, with such transcendant glory, that I cannot describe. My reader will please to take notice that this took place about midnight, and that the night was very dark, and that I did not see the vision with my natural eyes. At the instant that this glory opened on me, these words with their contents came with power to my soul:—"The times of refreshing are come from the presence of the Lord." Acts. iii.—19. And these words were also ushered in: "The Lord whom you seek, shall suddenly come to his temple;" Mal. iii.—1. and these also, "Behold me, behold me," Isa. lxv.—1. and immediately I felt a *rising* as sensibly as Lazarus did when he came out of the grave, and I am certain as sensibly as I shall do when the last trumpet shall be blown, and my dead body shall arise. O what a sudden coming of the Lord was here! What refreshings! and what a beholding, with wonder and astonishment! "What me, Lord?" I cried. "Yes, thee." "But I am unworthy, it cannot be, 'tis too great." I bowed down in myself and wondered, and wondered again, at so much goodness 'till I wept aloud, and cried like the prodigal, "Father, I have sinned against heaven, and in thy sight, and am no more worthy to be called thy son." Luke xv.—21. " I am unworthy of so much goodness." I then went to the window to see whether all was real, and whether I was rational. I could just see the trees, and perfectly well knew where I was, and that I was in my right mind. I then felt after the wrath of God but there was none. I felt after my guilt but all was gone. " The blood of Jesus Christ cleanseth us from all sin." 1 John i.—7. I felt after Moses in the curses of a broken law, but Moses was gone, and all his condemnings. "Who shall lay any thing to the charge of God's Elect? It is God that justifieth." Rom. viii.---33. I looked at justice, but he bade me claim my title to the tree of life. " Blessed are they that do his commandments, that they may have right to the tree of life." Rev. xxii.—14. " To him the porter openeth:

and the sheep hear his voice: and he calleth his own sheep by name, and leadeth them out." John x.—3. I looked for the guilt on my conscience, but conscience was silent being purged. I looked after the accuser of the brethren but he was gone, and the year of jubilee, " the acceptable year of the Lord" was come." Luke iv--19. I was free from wrath, free from guilt, free from the fear of death; "the lame man leaped as an hart, and the tongue of the dumb began to sing." Isa. xxxv.—6. O! this was " a morning without cloud," and I sung aloud of judgment past and mercy come. Psa. lix.—16. Now "the wilderness became like Eden, and the desert like the garden of the Lord." Isa. xxxi.—3. Now sprang up faith, hope, love, and joy, for the kingdom of God which is "righteousness and peace, and joy in the Holy Ghost," (Rom. xiv.—17.) was possessed by me. Now was " come Salvation, and strength, and the kingdom of our God, and the power of his Christ:" Rev. xii.—10. " I sat down under his shadow with great delight, and his fruit was sweet to my taste. He had brought me to the banqueting house, and his banner over me was love. "His left hand was under my head, and his right hand did embrace me." Songs ii.—3, 4, 6. His anger was all turned away, and nothing but love was now seen and felt. I drank of the river of his pleasure, and forgot my poverty, and remembered my misery no more. Prov.

xxxi.—7. Here was the law of release, and the law of kindness, and here was the perfect law of liberty. The spirit of life had made me free from the law of sin and death; and I cried out and said, "Now let thy servant depart in peace for mine eyes have seen thy Salvation," and like the mad Gadarene, "Let me go with thee Lord for I have seen and felt thy Salvation, for thou hast delivered my soul from death, and mine eyes from tears."

Here was sowing in tears and reaping in joy. The Apostle says that "we have redemption through his blood, the forgiveness of sins," Eph. i.—7. and I found it to be true. The Lord spake the word, and according to his promise, he spake it home to my heart; and said, "Deliver him from going down to the pit: I have found a ransom." Job xxxiii.—24. "And the ransomed of the Lord shall return, and come to Zion with songs and everlasting joy upon their heads: they shall obtain joy and gladness, and sorrow and sighing shall flee away." Isa. xxxv.---10.

About forty-eight hours after this took place, I was carried in the spirit, or in a trance, to a beautiful situation, were there was no person, besides myself, and as I was pleasantly amused and delighted, I sat me down with great delight: and a glorious person, who surpassed all my powers to describe, drew near and came up to me; he came from the east and passed toward the west; he stopped a little while, and smiled on me, which smile I shall never forget, or the raptures of joy that it communicated. He spake not, but cast into my lap a handful of nuts, but I was so taken with the glory of his person, that I had no thought of cracking the nuts. "He went down into the garden of nuts to see the fruits of the valley." Songs vi.---11. I knew not the vision at that time. Our Lord saith "What I do thou knowest not now; but thou shalt know hereafter." I now believe that these nuts set forth the promises, and dark portions of Holy Writ, and the dark providences that I should have to meet with; and truly I have found them to be like nuts, which are hard for little children to crack. The Apostle says that " when he was a child, he spake as a child, he understood as a child, and he thought as a child, but when he became a man he put away childish things;" and children need to be fed with milk, these being unable to crack nuts.

David speaks of having sworn enemies, and I do believe that I have some of this sort. Now I would ask these, what they *think* of this? I do not ask them what they *believe,* for I am fully persuaded that they never received so great a gift from God as a belief; for faith is the gift of God. Now, will you say in the light of the sun, that you ever knew the man? or that this is borrowed, or stolen, or that it was taught me by man? or will you say that 'tis all a delusion, and from the devil. I expect you will say the latter; not that I wish you so much ill, but I know you have been filling up the measure of your sins, some years past; and this, I have no doubt, in falling into your hands will occasion a great addition to that awful work, until you are full to the brim: for my Lord and master will not send you to your own place until this is the case with you. I pray God that if it be his will, you may be brought to repentance, for, if not, I am certain you will die in your sins, and where God is you never can come. John says that if a man hateth his brother and says that he loves God, he is a liar and the truth is not in him.

David in the joy of Salvation invites to come and taste and "see that the Lord is good," Psa. xxxiv.---8. and again, "come and hear, all ye that fear God (or love God) and I will declare what he hath done for my soul." Psa. lxvi.--16. I felt the same desire, and as I had been feasting on the mount and shouting from the tops of the hills, like those that are full of new wine, I longed to tell of it; and whom should I tell, but my teacher? Therefore I sat off to see Mr. Jenkins.

Now I have to inform my reader that I had never but once before had an interview with him: although I believe he never had a closer disciple than I had been for three years before that time: and that interview was not by a visit, but by accidentally meeting him near the Spring under the church-yard of the parish of Saint John in Lewes; he having heard of me was much pleased at meeting me and said that he should be obliged if I would favour him with my company: this I agreed to, and walked with him for about two hours, and we parted in great friendship. The reason of my not calling to see him was, not because of any coldness towards him, for the Lord knoweth that at that time he was my all, and my soul was knit to his, as Jonathan's was to David's; but I was so depressed with the thought and fear of some judgment falling on me, that I would not make myself familiar with him, lest his enemies should triumph and say, "there is one of his near friends;" and to have grieved him in that day would have been a double grief to me; and moreover I was naturally very shy. But now to see him I must go, in the hope of strengthening his hands, and off I went with a heart full to the brim; I had not then told any person of my deliverance as I meant that he should have the first fruits, not doubting of his having received of the same things in his own soul, but in this I was mistaken, for he knew nothing about them in the feeling enjoyment thereof at that time, but that I knew not until after this, when it appeared clearly to me by his own letters which I have in my own house to this day.

When I went to see him he was at the house of Mrs. Mockford, I asked for him, and as soon as I entered he saluted me with "well my old friend, how do you do?" My answer was, "Never so well before; who could have believed that God would have had such mercy on one so vile, so lost as I, as he has." I intended to to have told him the whole, but he broke in and stopped me, instead of drawing the matter out. Solomon says "wisdom in the heart of a man is like deep water, but a man of understanding will draw it out;" but this man had not this understanding at that time, and that you shall see: as I told you, he stopped me, and this was the way:---he broke out in anger and said that the devil, could give hope, and comfort people, whereby they might have much joy. This salutation to me was, like wrapping a cold wet cloth round a warm bosom; he never asked me the particulars of what had taken place, neither could I say any thing more of my own accord; for this was like an arrow shot in winged fowl, and I felt a pain at my heart: I therefore bade him good night, and left him.

The next evening he preached from this text, "The hope of the hypocrite shall be as the giving up of the Ghost;" and was very hot upon it, and declared that there was not one in that place that had a hope which was of God. Oh my feelings! how they were hurt.

Upon this there began to be a hue and cry about me, how that the devil had given me a deliverance; and the cry went through the troop of robbers: and their cry was like the cry in the days of Paul, when "they cried for the space of two hours, Great is Diana, but one half knew not what they meant;" and so it was here, for I was as close as a box, and gave no explanation, or reason of the hope that was in me, neither did they wish for it; I only said that I was delivered, and this was enough, all the dogs were set at me, in like manner as I have seen dogs set at beggars in a country town. One of the great ones told me to my face, that I must be wrong because Mr. Jenkins said so, and that if he was in my place, he would give all up for the sake of having peace and quietness, and begin again. This he might do I told him, but as for me I could do no such thing, for has it had been in times past so it was now; as in times past I could not lift myself up, so now I could not despair; and that I found that when the door of hope was opened to me, the door of despair shut: at this he left me. This man is still living, and so are several more of them, but when I chance to meet them, their downcast countenances declare that they still are in the bond of iniquity and the gall of bitterness, and I have no doubt of this being really the case with them. I certainly had felt a little pride, "and a haughty spirit goeth before a fall." Prov. xvi.—18. My sun shone so bright and clear, that I concluded my corruptions were all dead, and that I should see them no more.

"The sun ariseth, they gather themselves together, and lay them down in their dens." Psa. civ.—22.
But what with my pride, and what with these dogs constantly worrying me combined together, the enemy gained an advantage over me, and caused a doubt to arise which filled me with gloom, my old corruptions arose again. "Thou makest darkness, and it is night: wherein all the beasts of the forest do creep forth." Psa. civ.—20. I lost the light, the sweetness, and the joy that I had experienced, " my beloved had withdrawn himself, and was gone: I sought him, but I could not find him: I called him, but he gave me no answer." Cant. v.—6. This was a new trial to me, and I got into confusion, and found it to be true, that when he hideth himself, none can find him. The Minister could not describe my case, because at that time, he knew nothing of this in his own soul by feeling, so I wandered about and was like a locust, sometimes tossed up in hope and then down in doubt; the enemy worked powerfully to cause me to despair, but this he could not accomplish. I was cast down, but not in despair. How near the brink of it, I leave those that have been in the same trial to guess. There was no person that I knew, who had been in the same trial, therefore to me this was travelling alone in the dark. O how I fainted! like Jonah when the gourd withered, and the sun beat upon his head; and as he

wished in himself to die, so did I; for all were crying me down, and I was close shut up, and like the psalmist, I cried "bring my soul out of prison that I may praise thy name." Psa. cxlii.—7. The enemy followed me continually with the suggestion that I was like Saul, whom God forsook, and answered him not, neither by dreams, nor by vision, nor by prophets. 1 Sam. xxviii.—6. And that it was impossible for those who were once enlightened, and had tasted of the good word of God and the powers of the world to come, if they should fall away, that they should be saved, and also with this scripture, "destruction and misery are in their path."

In this trial I waded a whole year, all but a few days. One day as I was walking in a solitary place, much cast down and crying to the Lord to appear to my help, and telling the enemy that if my work was of the Lord, the Lord would certainly appear again, but if it was not of him the sooner I was cut out of the land of the living the better, for then my enemy would be at rest, and the important business would be settled; the Lord appeared and delivered me out of my distress. The enemy had long letten me with the 16th verse of the third chapter of the Epistle to the Romans, " Destruction and misery are in their ways." But now the Lord applied the 17th verse of the same chapter, with irresistible power, "and the way of peace have they not known." Such a precious light shone on me and on the word, that I saw that I had known the way of peace; and peace returned to me, and peace was proclaimed again. " He restored my soul," Psa. xxiii-3, and restored the joy of salvation again, so that I cried out aloud "this is my beloved, and this is my friend;" and leaped and jumped, and cried out " the devil is a liar, and his children are liars, but God is faithful and is come again, therefore I will doubt no more." Now my cup was full and run over with the good old wine of the kingdom. I was like a child who has been kept from the breast for a time, and Oh how it will suck when its little lips are favoured once more to take hold of the nipple! I cried " leave me not any more, and if thou wilt not, I will not care who leaves me, or despises me, for thou art my portion and my all in this world." Now I arose again in all the brightness of former times; here was being as the wings of a dove covered with silver. How clear I saw my interest in him again!

Now reader reflect what a trying state I had been in, there was no preaching to suit my case, or to cast the least ray of light on my path, no private person to drop a word for my help, but I was quite alone; you read that the Spirit led our Lord into the Wilderness, were he was forty days and forty nights tempted of the Devil, and was *alone,* and Angels came and ministered unto him. I became like a traveller who travels in a lonely path, and for fear of robbers keeps his treasure concealed and close: our Lord commands " not to cast your pearls before swine, lest they trample them under their feet, and turn again and rend you." Matt. vii.—6. The rough dealing that I have met with, has been the cause of my having hitherto kept these things so close; but all that the Lord has shewn me in secret, is in his own good time to be published on the house top; and that for two reasons; firstly, for the sake of those who may have to come after, and travel in the path of tribulation, as a light for them; and secondly, to stir up the wrath of man; and as it said that the enemies of Stephen gnashed on him with their teeth when he told them the truth, so this will help to fill up their measure that is wanting before they are cut off. After this, for some time, I continued walking amongst men, like the Apostle, "unknown, and yet well known," enduring many oppressions which fell to my lot.

I had for many years made up my mind (as I thought,) never to marry, yet I found some difficulty in escaping some, although I can say that I never gave them any cause, for I ever detested playing on the feelings of a female to gain her affections, and then abandoning her, I think it lets a man down very low, and renders him base; therefore I always stood clear of doing this; but on a certain day, I entered an house, and, as it was appointed before time, I saw her that is my present Wife, who being of the same profession, and going to the same place of Worship as myself, and being in modest dress, just to my taste, (for I have a great dislike to see the female that professes Godliness in gay attire, it certainly does not become such an one,) with one glance I was caught, and as she lived thirteen miles from this place, as soon as I had an opportunity, I told her of my desire to make her my wife, but that I did not wish to take her by surprize, neither to receive any answer at the present, and therefore I wished her to ask the Lord for counsel, and I would do the same; and would leave her to give me an answer at the end of three months. I saw her no more 'till the expiration of that time, and then we came to a decision, after which, we seldom saw each other oftener than once in four months; at length the time arrived that we were joined together in Holy Wedlock, but not without great opposition on the part of her friends.

This change in situation proved a thief to me, for the Creature robbed the Creator, and was the means, for a time, of cooling me towards my best friend. The Apostle says that we shall have trouble in the flesh, and so I found it, but I also found that the Apostle spared me, and did not tell of a tenth part of this trouble, for many were the troubles that fell to our lot, and I often concluded, more than my share; yet in the end they all worked for my good, and I have no reason to repent of any thing, either in my Courtship or Marriage, for the partner that the Lord alotted me, in the judgment of charity I conclude has been a very good one; I took her for a mixture, for better and for worse, and in this imperfect state, we shall find all women as well as men have their failings, as there is no perfection here, and so all will find it, and I can say with the poet,

> "What is the World and all things here?
> 'Tis but a bitter sweet;
> When I attempt a Rose to pluck,
> A pricking Thorn I meet.
> Here perfect bliss can ne'er be found,
> The Honey's mix'd with Gall."

This is all that is to be found in Creature, enjoyments on either side, male or female, and all sooner or later will say

> "Lord! what a wretched land is this,
> That yields us no supply;
> No cheering fruits, no wholesome trees,
> Nor streams of living joy"

But whether thy yoke be easy or galling, I would have thee remember that thy lot has fallen to thee according to the appointment and decree of the most high, and therefore refer thee to Paul's declaration, "the time is short: it remaineth, that both they that have wives be as though they had none; and they that weep, as though they wept not; and they that rejoice, as though they rejoiced not; and they that buy, as though they possessed not. 1 Cor. vii.--29, 30.

I found also that God would at all times be sought to for all things; oftentimes have I been compelled to ask of him for employment, and as often for strength to do it, as my health remains to this day in a very broken state. I have at times been compelled to beg and pray long for a situation or a house to live in, before I could obtain one; for I could not get any of these things without praying for them, and I advise thee, my reader, to carry all thy troubles to the same place, and ask, that thou mayest receive.

I shall now come to the time of the decline of the life of my pastor Mr. Jenkins; he was long infirm; and in the latter part of his life, one Mr. Hudson supplied his place occasionally. This man and I were on very friendly terms, and I greatly esteemed him for the work sake; for at the first he preached the law faithfully, and insisted on the death that would be felt by the coming of it; and on the power of God being felt to the bringing of the sinner from under the condemnation of it into the liberty of the gospel. In this was the very life of my soul, and I felt my heart closely attached to him.

But some may say "Was there not some coldness between you before he left Lewes?" I answer, There was. For I loved him for the truth's sake, and not merely for his amiable qualities as a man, as many did; and latterly he began to decline and swerve from the truth, and to build up what he had before pulled down. The Apostle says that such a man is a transgressor, and whenever this takes place we are justified in separating from that man, as the Apostle separated from Dimas or Philetus. But before we parted, being grieved, I called upon him several times, and conversed freely with him on these things; but still he kept wavering and reeling, and I saw clearly that it was in vain to endeavour to keep a man to the truth, except the Lord keeps him to it; for he will surely fall a reeling again, in spite of all any man can do by admonition or counsel to prevent it.

This man was a collector of the excise, and the Board soon after the death of Mr. Jenkins ordered him away from Lewes, and stationed him at Manchester. The Board of Excise, I own, were the secondary cause of his removal, but I hold the Lord to be the first cause, and did believe then, and so I do now, that, although a good man, the Lord banished him from Lewes, for this, his dissimulation and not being faithful to the trust of the gospel.

There was one man that stood high in Mr. Hudson's recommendation, and when I called on the latter to bid him farewell, I asked him whether he had received this man in the manifestation of the spirit, according to his own light of a brother; and he confessed that he had not, neither could he, but only as a friend. Oh what unfaithfulness and cowardice was here! The conduct of this man grieved me sore, and I cried out all these things are against me, and "I saw all Israel scattered upon the hills, as sheep that have not a shepherd." 1 Kings xxii.—17. I cried to the Lord to look on our afflictions, and these words came to me with an irresistable energy and power, "I have put my words in thy mouth," "and thou shalt go to all that I shall send thee." Jer. i.—9, 7. I replied, I cannot go, I cannot go, I have no abilities, I have no memory, fit for so great a work, spare me. But these words followed up, "Whatsoever I command thee that thou shalt speak. Be not afraid of their faces: for I am with thee to deliver thee, saith the Lord, Jer. i.—7, 8, and "When he saw the multitudes, he was moved with compassion on them, because they fainted, and were scattered abroad, as sheep having no shepherd. Then saith he unto his disciples, the harvest truly is plenteous, but the labourers are few." Matt. ix.—36, 37. I felt the word burn like fire within me; and like Elihu "I was full of matter, the spirit within me constrained me. My belly was as wine which had no vent; it was ready to burst like new bottles," so that I was constrained "to speak, that I might be refreshed; to open my lips and answer." Job xxxii.—18, 20.

I told no man of this vision, but like Mary pondered all these things in my heart, wondering what it all meant: and as for my own choice, I can truly say, I was the last in my own eyes; I would have caught at any one before myself: but the Lord is of one mind, and no one can turn him, and he giveth not account of any of his matters. Job xxiii.—13.

At a meeting of a few in my own house I felt a springing up, and spake out as the Lord gave me utterance. Peter saith, "As every man hath received the gift, even so minister the same one to another, as good stewards of the manifold grace of God. If any man speak, let him speak as the oracles of God; if any man minister, let him do it as of the ability which God giveth." 1 Peter iv.—10, 11.

I felt something like Moses, when "he supposed his brethren would have understood how that God by his hand would deliver them:" Acts vii.—25, for I had no doubt but that a few of my old friends would have been pleased, and would strengthen my hands and say, God speed, but Oh what a great mistake! instead of that, they soon began to shew their great alarm for fear that if I preached so close and so rousing a doctrine I should set the whole town on fire. These were their own words, let them deny them if they can. They shortly all forsook me.

I pray God that it may not be laid to their charge. Notwithstanding the Lord stood with me, and strengthened me. 2 Tim. iv.—16, 17. Therefore I continued speaking in my own house.

A little before this time we became acquainted with M'Culla; which acquaintance caused me many a sorrow, I shall relate it, as briefly as I can in truth, that others may take the Apostle's advice, to " lay hands suddenly on no man," 1 Tim. v.—22. and the exhortation, to "make no friendship with an angry man, and with a furious man not to go." Prov. xxii.—24.

This acquaintance began about, or near the time of the death of Mr. Jenkins; M'Culla came to Brighton to preach, several persons went from Lewes to hear him, amongst whom I was one; and I and some others could but say that he preached the truth and divided the law from the gospel, and insisted on the application of both. The next time that we went to hear him, we had an interview with him; and there appeared in him no bitterness, nor wrath, but quite the reverse: he appeared as harmless as a lamb or a dove. " Beware of false prophets, which come to you in sheep's clothing, but inwardly they are ravening wolves." Matt. vii.—15. He declared that he only sought the good of the children of Israel. " The simple believeth every word:" Prov. xiv.—15. " With her much fair speech she caused him to yield, with the flattering of her lips she forced him." Prov. vii.—21. So it happened with some of us that we were taken in this net, not taking the Apostle's advice to lay hands suddenly on no man. I for one acknowledge that I caught hold of this man too soon. "Why wilt thou my son, be ravished with a strange woman, and embrace the bosom of a stranger," Prov. v.—20. and for this I for one have smarted sorely.

It has been said that we invited him to come to Lewes, the first time, but this was not the fact. He came without inviting. A letter was sent to us, desiring us to get a place if possible in which he might preach. What do you call this but creeping into houses? And 'tis well known to you since, that he led captive silly women.

He next urged us to get a place for him to preach in once a month : upon which eleven of us agreed with a builder to build one, and to let it to us on a lease for seven years, and at a meeting of the eleven, it was agreed that M'Culla should have forty shillings and his board every time he came, and whatever might be collected at the door of the meeting-house besides; and that he should have no controul, power, or command over us, or in ordering of any thing amongst us, or over the meeting-house, but that all order and rule should be in the majority of the eleven. This was agreed to without a dissentient voice, and appeared to be a sure binding.

Thus we set sail on this stormy ocean, as it proved to be indeed by what followed.

When we entered this new chapel we left my house in which I had continued to speak up to this time twice a day: and when we were about to move, I informed them that I should decline speaking twice a day, and should only speak once a day in the new meeting-house; lest any should be jealous of my usurping too much over them, as a little of that already began to appear; and that I should leave it to their own choice whether any one of them should speak on the other part of the day. I thought this would have given full content, but not so; although one of them took on him to speak on one part of the day, it did not last long before jealousy began to work on this point. When the time came that I should speak, many people would come to hear, but when my partner occupied, but a very few would attend. I could not help this, I always was there; and I can say, that not only then but to this day, I never pressed nor asked any one to come to hear me, and I hope I never shall, as there is no need of that, the Lord takes this in his own hands; "For he shall gather them as the sheaves into the floor. Arise and thrash, O daughter of Zion: for I will make thine horn iron, and I will make thy hoofs brass: and thou shalt beat in pieces many people." Micah. iv.—12, 13.

Therefore that the honour of these men might

not be lost, they purposed that I should not speak on any set part of the day, lest the people should come at that time only; and therefore it was appointed that I should not myself know on what part of the day I was to occupy until I saw the other man arise and begin, or he gave me the command to do so. To this arrangement I yielded without a reply, in the hope that this would have made quietness.

But this, alas, did continue but a very short time before I was charged with different crimes, and summoned to appear before the great tribunal of these men, in which M'Culla was to be the judge, and ten men were to be both the witnesses against me and the jury to try me.

Accordingly the judgment was set, and up came the trembling prisoner. I was charged by one evil surmiser with three things:—first, that I was a disaffected person to the king; secondly, that I was a rogue; and thirdly, that I did not preach clearly the spirit's work in a sinner's heart. Could any man be charged with greater evils than I was charged with? It was asked of me, whether I would vindicate myself; I replied that I would on the two first charges: which I think I did to the full satisfaction of that evil court, so that they were ashamed of my accuser. Of the third charge I declined to vindicate myself, as I considered that they ought to be the best judges on that point. This question was therefore put to them singly: "Does

Master Gibbs speak consistently with the Spirit's Work, or no?" The first said that he could not say I did not. The next said that he could not say I did not. The third spake greatly in my praise, but was soon bid by the judge to hold his tongue. You are to understand that the man who thus spake in my favour, was the greatest man amongst them. And now as my trial began to stop I expected that the evidence would have been cast up, and that I should have been discharged; but no, the judge instead of taking any review of the evidence flew at me himself, and asked me whether I took a whole chapter and explained it all through. My answer was "No." "Then how do you do?" I replied "I dare do no such thing, I am so dark, and have such trembling before I begin that I often conclude that I shall have nothing to say, for the book is sealed, but just as the time comes, a part of a verse, or a small sentence offers itself, and a small light dawns on it, and I go forth; and at times it increases 'till I am full." Now comes my sentence: "Master Gibbs, this is wrong altogether, and if God had called you to preach, you would be able to take a whole chapter and explain it all through, and have no trembling." Well, thought I, if that be right I am altogether wrong. Thus the trial ended, and in a short time after, I was forbidden by M'Culla to speak in the little chapel. I then returned to speak in my own house as I had done before to those that desired to hear me.

Then M'Culla's people called upon me to fulfil the former agreement to pay part of the rent of the chapel, this I declined to do on this ground, that they had broken the agreement, and fallen off the foundation first laid down, in giving up the command of the chapel into the hands of M'Culla, and therefore I contended that the agreement as to me was null and void altogether; and before long M'Culla shut them all out of the chapel, and they dared not to go there any more than myself; and after a little while longer it was shut up altogether: so that for several years they paid the rent, although they had no preaching in it.

Now I was called and blasted with all the bad names that malice could invent, and in order to be avenged of me, all of them, except one, took away their work from me, which was a great loss to me at that time. Now my reader, all this is true. What think you of this treatment? Was I right? or was I wrong? I would not wish to be first in my own cause.

This same M'Culla made his boast that he would preach my Funeral Sermon, and that he would never cease pursuing me till I was lodged in the pit of hell with the prince of rebels. Some of his disciples have denied this; but I have his letter in my house to this day, in his own hand writing, in which I can shew it verbatim. I concluded in that day, that if this man had ever been in the feelings I had been in, he would never have wished the worst enemy he had in this world to have felt the same, much less to be lodged in hell itself. This convinced me that he knew nothing about hell or the pains of it; if he had, he would not have wished to lodge me there. The Lord by Moses says that "if a prophet speaketh in the name of the Lord, if the thing follow not, nor come to pass, that is the thing which the Lord hath not spoken, but the prophet hath spoken it presumptuously: thou shalt not be afraid of him." Deut. xviii.—22. Now who will presume to say that this man's prophesying came to pass. Hath not the Lord cut him out of the land of the living, and still spared me, although I acknowledge that I am an unprofitable servant? "The wicked watcheth the righteous, and seeketh to slay him. The Lord will not leave him in his hand, nor condemn him when he is judged. Wait on the Lord, and keep his way, and he shall exalt thee to inherit the land: when the wicked are cut off, thou shalt see it. The transgressors shall be destroyed together: the end of the wicked shall be cut off." Psa. xxxvii.—32, 34, 38. "They are exalted for a little while, but are gone and brought low; they are taken out of the way as all other, and cut off as the tops of the ears of corn. And if it be not so now, who will make me a liar, and make my speech nothing worth?" Job xxiv.—24, 25.

Now I will shew my reader how the anger of this man first began to break out against me. As one day he and I were alone, he asked me what I thought of Mr. Huntington; I told him I believed him to be a great man and a good man. At this he was chafed, and appeared bitter, and declared that Mr. H. would be damned, and so would all his adherents except they gave him up. This I told him I could not do, for if I gave him up, I must give up him (M'Culla) also, for I had not received so great a proof of him, as I had of Mr. Huntington, and that the reason of my thus holding of Mr. H. was this:---at three different times since my deliverance, I had been in great darkness and doubt, as to my interest in the friend of sinners, and no man's word was ever so blessed to me in those days as was his, especially at three different times never to be forgotten. This had given him a place in my heart never to be dislodged again; and as I never had any acquaintance with him personally, I knew it must have come immediately from God. I acknowledged that he was not without his failings any more than other good men, but that I knew that God had spoken through him to my heart; and I said to M'Culla "if this is not a witness for him, I know I can have no witness for you, as I never had such a witness for you." This great man, at this simple answer was beaten, but from that time he held a grudge against me and never could he rest until he avenged himself of me, by prejudicing the minds of all my friends against me.

When I first began to speak I was in hopes that all my brethren would have succoured me by their counsel, advice, prayers, and sympathy; but God's ways are not as our ways, nor his thoughts as our thoughts; instead of giving me help by friendship, they turned to be my bitter enemies, and declared that if I preached so close a doctrine I should set all the town on fire; so that I may truly say with the Apostle, "At my first answer no man stood with me but all forsook me: I pray God that it may not be laid to their charge." 2 Tim. iv.—16.

Nevertheless, the Lord soon caused his word to enter the heart of one who had been a stranger to me, and this man abode with me in my first days, and would not let me sink, but by hearty counsel and with a firm faith, exhorted me to persevere, predicting of the blessings that would crown my labours. "The Lord give mercy unto the house of Onesiphorus, for he oft refreshed me, and was not ashamed of my chain: the Lord grant unto him, that he may find mercy of the Lord in that day." 2 Tim. i. —16, 18. Many times in my temptations was this friend made useful to me, to succour me, and to strengthen my hands, Exod. xvii.—12, and to this day I consider him as one of my worthies, and shall do so as long as life lasts. 2 Sam. xxiii.—15, 16.

I have related, that I returned to my own house to preach as I had done before. In my own house I continued to preach for the space of two years more; many afflictions I waded through during this time, I was in a very weak and sickly state of health, I had a heavy family, my little business was blown on by the wind of persecution, till there was nothing for me to look forward to but abject poverty; and now this question was often put, "Will you look back? you have put your hand to the plough, and the wind of adversity blows right in your face: but if you turn back in this stormy day, woe be to you; and if you persevere, woe will be to you and all your family, for both you and they will be brought to the Workhouse?" I kept this concealed from all men, and at times felt this determination, that whether I sink or swim I will leave all to the Lord, and if I sink I have deserved to do worse.

In my first preaching, I was much indulged of the Lord, he gave me easily a text with a little light and sweetness; I concluded that this in future would increase, and thought how pleasant preaching would be in a future day; truly I thought as a child, for instead of this being the case, the light withdrew, and the word closed, and often I could not get a text;

then instead of sweetness, I felt bitterness, and cried out, " woe is me, my leanness, my leanness." Now I was heavily tempted and tried, and the enemy thus pushed at me, "*you* called to the office of a preacher, you feel like it, do you not? Who so empty as you, who so dark, and who so destitute of dew and of the excellency of the power as you? There is no springing up of the water of life, all is dry, and so it will always remain. The enemies will shout as they did in the days of Samson, and God's little few will be ashamed."

I have begged of the Lord to suffer every person to be so prejudiced, that not one might come to hear me, then I should be at a point that the Lord had not called me to preach, and I have waited with a longing desire and expectation for my prayer to be thus answered; but instead of that, at the regular time the door has opened as usual, the sound whereof, will never be forgotten by me, Oh! with what pain has it thus spoke to my heart, "now you must come down and speak:" so that I have trembled all over and been in a cold sweat.

At other times I have begged of the Lord, that if *he* had not sent me, he would lay some great affliction on me, so as to confine me to my bed, then it would be all over and the doubtful point be settled. At other times I have begged of him, that if he intended I should preach, he would in his providence send me to a great distance from Lewes; as I considered that in Lewes, were some of the clearest and brightest persons in judgment, and yet the greatest hypocrites in heart, of any in all England; but I found that in this also the purposes of the Lord shall stand, and he will do all his pleasure, and that, "he is of one mind, and who can turn him? and what his soul desireth, even that he doeth." Job xxiii—13.

When I have been thus tossed about and tried, I have at the last moment found a sentence with a small ray of light on it, which, like the little cloud that appeared to the prophet's servant, at first of the size of a man's hand, has increased 'till it has covered the Heavens, causing me to cry out, "Lord it is enough," I will doubt no more; and like Peter have said, "It is good to be here." But soon have I fell to doubting again. Yet I can say, that for the most part, the more I have been tempted and tried, the sweeter has the time of preaching that has followed it been, and the more refreshing. I find the preparation of the heart, as well as the answer of the tongue, is from the Lord. Being but a babe in the ministry, I had not arrived at Paul's exhortation to his Son, to "be instant in Season, and out of Season." 2 Tim. iv,—2. I felt it pleasant, to preach in season: but out of season when all was dark, when heavily tempted, and the Lord hid himself, both in providence, and in his gracious favour, and almost all men were crying out "he hath a devil and is mad, why do ye hear him?" And all that did hear, suffered the loss of their good name; and if in the habit of receiving any favours, either in gifts or trade, they were made to suffer the loss thereof; looking at the things that were seen, I often fainted, and like Jonah wished to die.

In these days M'Culla and another great Minister declared that God had not sent me to preach, and gave this as a proof of it, that I had no place to preach in; and that if God had called me to the work of his ministry, he would have provided a place for me. How astonishing this was to me. It was the very temptation wherewith the enemy was afflicting me and dragging me through within, that these men spake of without. This I then wondered at, as I knew that I never had mentioned it to any person, although the truth was, that I from month to month had doubted of all on this very account. But I have since seen the same thing in Job, the very temptation that he laboured under in his own soul, the enemy caused his wife to try him with. Job ii.—9.

In this trial, like Gideon who begged that the floor might be dry and the fleece wet, and then that the fleece might be dry and the floor wet, to confirm his doubtful mind; so I often asked the Lord not to let any one come to hear me, except that it was his pleasure that I should preach, and if any one came that he would give me at the last moment a sentence, or a small part of his word with light thereon and dew, and I would believe that it was his pleasure. This he often was pleased to do, so as to astonish me; yet all this would not do entirely to remove my scruples; therefore I tried him with this request "O Lord, if thou hast appointed me to speak in thy great name, give me this proof also, give me only an empty room to hire in some house." And this I would observe, that none can know how inconvenient and trying it is to preach, shut up in a little house with a large family, but those that have proved it; neither do I wish any to know one tenth part of my sufferings in that situation. I was determined not to make known my desire respecting this matter to any man, that I might see clearly the Lord's hand in the matter.

After this had passed between the Lord and me, I was surprised with the visit of a friend who had received the word in the love of it, whose errand was to inform me that the Lord had sent him to provide a place for the Lord's word to be spoken in. "Commit thy way unto the Lord; trust also in him; and he shall bring it to pass." Psa. xxxvii.—5. I had been enabled to commit this into his hand, and found this portion of the Lord's word to be true, "Thy Father which seeth in secret shall reward thee openly," Matt. vi.---6. for now the Lord began to reward me openly.

For this friend, whom I hope ever to esteem as an instrument in the Lord's hand, and as one who has followed the Apostle's exhortation to his son, "Not to be ashamed of the testimony of the Lord, nor of his servant: but to be a partaker of the afflictions of the gospel according to the power of God." 2 Tim. i.—8. I have reason to bless the Lord: and that he enabled him to suffer reproach and persecution for the love that he bore to the Lord's cause; and as the Apostle said to his son, "This thou knowest, that all they which are in Asia be turned away from me; of whom are Phygellus and Hermogenes. The Lord give mercy unto the house of Onesiphorus; for he oft refreshed me, and was not ashamed of my chain: but when he was in Rome, he sought me out very diligently, and found me; 2 Tim. i.—15, 16, 17. so I can truly say of this man, and more also, the 18th verse "The Lord grant unto him that he may find mercy of the Lord in that day: and in how many things he ministered unto me, thou knowest very well," and that on account of the Lord's cause only, as I was not in the habit of receiving favours on my own account, but was determined to sink or swim according as it might be my Lord's will. It is said of Moses that he chose rather to suffer affliction with the people of God, than to enjoy the pleasures of sin for a season. Heb. xi.—25.

But my reader may reply, and say that there is no suffering for a profession in our day. I agree with him that it is so, if it be only an empty profession of Christ in the flesh, 2 Cor. v.—16. with this Christ there is honour, profit, esteem, and worldly gain. How many are much better off for their profession than they were before, how much good have these reaped in the things of this life. This is a " golden slipper day" indeed. Their fear is taught by the precepts of man. Take away your favours, and you will soon have a discovery of those that follow for the loaves and fishes; and I am fully persuaded that some of you who have this world's goods in your hands know in your breasts this to be true; take away all your gifts and favours, and you lose your disciples; but heap to them and they will cleave close to you and cry you up. But you may say, are we not to do good? I answer yes, and to communicate, but not to the purchasing of empty hypocrites to make a large congregation. I mistake, if some do not have to rue for this another day. You may cry out "The grapes are sour." Well, I know that I and my few friends have it not in our power to give gifts, and I have reason to thank God that it is not in our power, for by this I have a clearer proof and am certain that no wordly interest brings or can bring us a disciple, and I hope that no one may be so tempted to cast in their lot with us.

You may make a great ado about what is called gospel, and be very full of zeal, and be highly approved by man, although an abomination to God. But not if you declare how the law cut you down so that you was without hope and without a claim on the Lord, and that there was none shut up, or left; Deut. xxxii.—36. that then the Lord fulfilled his promise, and manifested himself to you in his gracious favour, as he does not to the worldly professor; which is being called by his grace and having his dear Son revealed in you, which will be the hope of glory. And when this Revelation takes place you will say, "I have the knowledge of Salvation by the Forgiveness of my Sins," and all your guilt will be removed from off your conscience; all fear, wrath, anger, and fearfulness of the Day of Judgment will pass away as waters, and will no more be found as they have been before; which if you are a stranger to, I exhort you not to speak evil of, lest your bands should be made strong, and you be made to dwell in a barren land; for it would have been better for you if you had never been born, than that you should die a stranger to this: and if you have known this, with the mouth you must confess it to the glory of God; and when you do this and insist that all others must pass through death, before they come to the enjoyment of life, you will find what suffering will follow; men and devils will pursue you, and your name will be cast out as evil and as dangerous to society; and they will speak all manner of evil of you falsely for his name sake, and they that see you without will flee from you, Psa. xxxi.—11. and the more sanctity they have in their appearance, yet being destitute of this work of the spirit, the more will they persecute you, and shoot their arrows in secret Psa. lxiv.—3. to wound your name and reputation, and cry out " this man is not fit to be a minister ; away with such a fellow, for he hurts the feelings of the humble and the sincere seeker, and all the little ones; instead of which he ought to preach comfort to all these."

Let such remember that man is not to teach God, but God will teach man ; " For who hath known the mind of the Lord ? or who hath been his counsellor ? Or who hath first given to him, and it shall be recompensed unto him again?" Rom. xi.—34, 35. He that separates the precious from the vile shall be as his mouth. "The voice saith, cry. And the obedient cryer saith, What shall I cry ? " All flesh is grass, and all the goodliness thereof is as the flower of the field: the grass withereth, the flower fadeth: because the spirit of the Lord bloweth upon it: surely the people is grass." Isa. xl.—6, 7. He that preaches death by a broken law, and life by the proclamation of the year of release or jubilee; God's mercy and grace revealed by the spirit of life in Christ Jesus, to give freedom to those that are bound : does the work of an Evangelist. This is not rising up early and blessing his friend, Prov. xxvii.—14. as many have done, and it has proved a curse to them, as may be seen to this day.

And as for those they call sincere, or as having a desire, I pay no regard to ; for I read that there are those that desire, and have nothing, Prov. xiii—4. but the approbation of man; and that "many will seek to enter in, and shall not be able," Luke xiii.—23, 24, for it is not of him that willeth, nor of him that runneth, but to whom God will shew mercy. Rom. ix.---16.

And as for the little ones that most men talk of, I consider that he is one of Solomon's valiant men, expert in war, and whose sword is girt upon his thigh that dasheth such against the stones. Psa. cxxxvii.—9. For I consider one of these to be only a name without a reality, or a nonentity, neither brought forth nor begotten; for the Lord has said, "I will greatly multiply thy sorrow and thy conception;" Gen. iii.—16. and if these had been begotten again by the word of truth, great sorrow would have been the attendant of it, and spiritual travail, and crying out for want of strength to bring forth ; "He giveth power to the faint ; and to them that have no might he increaseth strength." Isa. xl.—29.

As many as receive Christ, receive him in

receiving the truth that is against them, and yet in the love of that truth : and as the flaming sword which kept the way of the Tree of Life, lest man should put forth his hand and take and live, Gen. iii.—24. so are " his Ministers a flaming fire." Psa. civ.—4. To such as thus receive the truth, he gives power to claim what they were born heirs to; that is, to say " My Father." Because we are sons by predestination. He has sent the spirit into our hearts to bear witness with our spirits that we are sons of God, and to cry " Abba Father." Now I consider that no person has any warrant to palm any upon God, as his children until this has taken place, nor to claim God as their God. And woe be to that man that doeth the work of God deceitfully. Jer. xlviii.—10. This is a little one, who has thus been brought forth; and he is said to suck at the breast, and to be dandled on the knee, and borne on the side, and be abundantly satisfied and delighted with the abundance of Zion's Glory. Isa. lxvi.—11.

This sucking child is to play on the hole of the asp, Isa. xi.—8. which reptile is very full of bitter poison; and whom does this reptile represent, but a professor who has never been delivered either from the guilt of sin or the power and dominion of it : and when he hears a poor sinner confess with the mouth unto so great a Salvation as to be delivered from all this; his secret venom is stirred up, and his countenance proclaims it, and he waits to shoot his arrows, even bitter words.

Now I ask, can there be in any house or family, a lesser branch or twig or character than this child that I have described? John says, "I write unto you, little children, because your sins are forgiven you;" and I know that I dared not claim my sonship until my guilt was removed from my conscience, although I know now, that I was a son before time, according to predestination.

But after this comes the time to be weaned, the breast of consolation and of sweet joy is taken from the child, and the feasting days are over, and he "shall desire to see one of the days of the son of man, and shall not see it." Luke xvii.—22. This question is put, "Whom shall he teach knowledge? And whom shall he make to understand doctrine? Them that are weaned from the milk, and drawn from the breasts." Isa. xxviii.—9. The Apostle Peter says, "Grow in Grace and in the knowledge of our Lord and Saviour Jesus Christ." 2 Peter iii.—18. and the Apostle Paul says, that he became a man. 1 Cor. xiii.—11. And John says I write to you young men, because ye have overcome the wicked one, 1 John ii.—14. and then he writes to the fathers.

Now I would ask my opponents, whether this is being born six feet high, as they represent the minister of truth to preach as being the case? O what dark shades and misrepresentations they draw and make, to prejudice the minds of the simple and the unwary! The same trials I observe fell to the lot of the psalmist, " the mouth of the wicked and the mouth of the deceitful are opened against me: they have spoken against me with a lying tongue. They compassed me about also with words of hatred; and fought against me without a cause." Psa. cix.—2, 3. " Deliver my soul, O Lord, from lying lips, and from a deceitful tongue. What shall be given unto thee? or what shall be done unto thee, thou false tongue? Sharp arrows of the mighty, with coals of juniper." Psa. cxx.—2, 4. I admonish you to consider the consequences, and to weigh well what is said in the Epistle of Jude, "Behold, the Lord cometh with ten thousand of his Saints, to execute judgment upon all, and to convince all that are ungodly among them of all their ungodly deeds which they have ungodly committed, and of all their hard speeches which ungodly sinners have spoken against him." verses—14, 15.

Well this friend, whose errand I have related, desired me to take the business into my own hands for reasons best known to himself, and to go for him to hire or buy, whichever I could, a fit place: I wished to hire rather than buy. Hereupon I took a circuit all round the town: (I have often thought that my case was much like Nehemiah's, and if you read the second chapter of Nehemiah you may see a striking likeness) but after roaming several times around and through the town, all was denied me. I thought that I would call on Mrs. Mantell and ask her whether she had let her school-room in Saint John-street for any length of time; upon this impulse I called on her; and I speak it to her honour, that no person could have behaved with greater generosity than she did to me: she told me that the place was let, but for no longer than by the year, and that if I wanted it to preach in she would immediately give the tenant notice to quit, and let it to me: I thanked her for her kindness, and told her that I could not accept of so great a favour on such bad ground as to be the means of turning out the present tenant, for if I did, I should expect that the cause would not prosper, therefore I had rather decline the place altogether: she then advised me to call on the tenant (as there could be no harm in doing that) and ask him whether it was his wish to give up the place. I took this counsel, and called on the tenant and asked him; and his answer was immediate and short, " How could you think that I could give up the place, as I want it for my manufactory as it just suits me." I begged his pardon, and hoped that he would not be offended with me, as I did but just ask him: he did not know any thing of my having been to his landlady.

I returned home with a heart full of trouble, as it could hold; the enemy suggesting that all hope of my obtaining a place was over, for no one would let me any, neither would they sell me any; and that my enemies prophesied in triumph. O what labour I found to bring my will to resign. But after many a cry, the Lord sent me resigning grace; and after the storm was quelled, there came a deliverance never to be forgotten by me; for on the afternoon of the second day after, a person wrapped at my door, I arose from my work to open the door, and to my great surprise it was the very man who the other day answered me roughly: he now began by saying "Sir, you called on me the other day to ask me whether I should have any objection to give up that building; I am come to tell you, that if you like to have it I will give it up to you, and will give the key to you now, so that before my goods are taken out you may send persons to repair it, as it is greatly out of order." Now reader, this man was a total stranger to me; therefore what must my feelings be upon hearing this, surely something like Joseph's when he turned aside to weep, and so did I, before I could give him an answer; but although I was greatly abashed, after a short time I resumed courage, and turned round and received the key from him, and thanked him kindly for the favour he had thus shewed me.

Those that have plenty of wealth and of wealthy friends may laugh at this which they may call simple stuff: but let them be as destitute of these things as I have been, then I believe they will not make a puff at them; therefore I will answer them with the words of the wise man: "The wise man's wealth is his strong city: the destruction of the poor is their poverty." Prov. xi—15. And again, "The rich man's wealth is his strong city, and as an high wall in his own conceit." Prov. xviii.—11.

I soon repaired to the landlady, and agreed to become a yearly tenant of the place: and I can truly say that for some years I added money out of my own hard labour to help pay the rent of it: but some may say, would not the people pay the rent? In answer to which, consider how few there were to pay, as this house was too large by above two parts out of three for the number that then assembled: and lest we should be ashamed, I had it parted into two, and then the part we occupied was too large by half: and another thing, I had rather preach for nothing, and pay part of the rent and do all the service of the house myself, than let either friend or foe see the "Nakedness of the Land;" and I can truly say that I did it willingly for the love I had to my master and his truth: "if I forget thee O Jerusalem, let my right hand forget her cunning. If I do not remember thee, let my tongue cleave to the roof of my mouth; if I prefer not Jerusalem above my chief joy." Psa. cxxxvii.—5, 6. and the Lord knoweth it before whom I stand.

I furnished the house with the meanest furniture, it being only old barrack seats without backs, and a pulpit made of boards in their rough state without being planed: O my children, in a future day remember how low I began, and be not ashamed of the place, nor of me, your spiritual father. "Look unto the rock whence ye are hewn, and to the hole of the pit whence ye are digged. Look unto Abraham your father, and unto Sarah that bare you: for I called him alone, and blessed him and increased him." Isa. li.—1, 2.

Upon every little prosperity that attended, I by degrees, garnished the house; I rejoiced and yet I had a secret trembling, although I kept it close; which arose from this thought: suppose an enemy that has got money, and many of them have, should, to avenge themselves of me, buy the house over our head, what a pretty figure we shall cut in packing out our old stuff: what a laughing, what a jeering, and what a sneering there will be. The devil set all this before me, and often in imagination dragged me through the dirty places. In this trial I often in secret intreated the Lord to put it into the heart of some friend to buy the house to ease me of the fear that thus oppressed me; and in the Lord's time this was done; for the old friend called on me and said that his mind was uneasy through fear that some evil-minded enemy should buy the house and turn us out.

Here I saw the Lord's hand clearly, as I had

never mentioned my fears or wishes on the subject either to this friend or to any one else. What a mercy it is, when we are enabled to commit our ways unto the Lord. "Trust in the Lord, and do good; so shalt thou dwell in the land, and verily thou shalt be fed. Delight thyself also in the Lord; and he shall give thee the desires of thine heart. Commit thy way unto the Lord; trust also in him; and he shall bring it to pass." Psalms xxxvii.—3, 5. O how often have I found the Lord's time to be the best time; all secondary causes then concur to fulfil his decreed purposes; therefore one says, " he performeth the thing that is appointed for me : and many such things are with him." Job. xxiii.—14.

My friend required *me* to go and make the purchase, which was rather trying to me, as I was totally unacquainted with the buying of property. I begged of the Lord to over rule all the bargain, and sure enough he did; for just at that time, in consequence of family arrangements, a sale of the property was to be made; and after some little treaty with my landlady, I made a final agreement with her for the purchase.

I at that time did not know whether it was a good bargain or not, but upon afterwards calling on the late Mr. Thomas Woollgar, whose great knowledge of the value of property was exceeded by few; he told me that there had not been so advantageous a purchase made in Lewes lately, and that some time before, himself had offered considerably more money for it than I had agreed to give. This caused my heart to melt in gratitude.

Now I had a new landlord, but before the conveyance to him was completed, an evil minded person, (not knowing what had taken place) went to my old landlady and offered to purchase the whole; whence my reader may see in what a crisis we purchased the house, and how near my fears were realised; but what says the royal Psalmist, "He that sitteth in the Heavens shall laugh: the Lord shall have them in derision," Psa. ii.—4, and, "the wicked plotteth against the just, and gnasheth upon him with his teeth. The Lord shall laugh at him: for he seeth that his day is coming. The wicked have drawn out the sword, and have bent their bow, to cast down the poor and needy, and to slay such as be of upright conversation." Psa. xxxvii.—12, 14.

Now then, my reader may be ready to say, as your friend was become your landlord you were quite at ease about the place? I answer, no, for the enemy pushed at me on another quarter, and raised these thoughts, suppose another King should arise, that knows not Joseph. Exod. i.—8 How will it be then? Why out you must turn, and have to face the scorn of all your enemies.

My reader may say, "how full of unbelief

you must be, that you could not trust God for a place to speak his word in." I confess that all this is true indeed, I am full of unbelief; and that counterbalances my faith, and oftentimes overtops it: and as my faith was given me by God, and wrought in me by the spirit, I find that the acting of that faith depends on the influence of the spirit, and that " I believe, according to the working of his mighty power." Ephes. i.—19. So when the influence is strong, the acting of my faith is strong also; but when the influence is withdrawn, then many doubts arise: " In my prosperity I said, I shall never be moved. Lord, by thy favour thou hast made my mountain to stand strong: thou didst hide thy face, and I was troubled." Psa. xxx.—6, 7. I see this also in the prophet Elijah; for who so bold and courageous in the matter of the slaying of the prophets of Baal as he; and who had so clear a display of God's presence and approbation as he, when fire came down on the burnt offering and consumed all: but look at 1 Kings xix.—2, 3, and you will see that upon the threat of a wicked woman all his faith failed him, and he fled for his life. I do not profess to have a faith and have no doubtings; I would to God that I had, if it was consistent with his will; but I find that it is not: I find that unbelief is the sin that so easily besets me, and often makes me groan under these two burthens, the whole body of sin that plunges and struggles for the mastery, and unbelief. Here I find is no rest; but being blessed with a hope that is full of immortality, I am looking for a complete rest without alloy.

My old friend called on me one day and said that he was not quite at rest about the little chapel; I began to wonder what the matter could be, as I always paid him the rent with a great deal of pleasure every half year, and I had no idea what his uneasiness was about: but he soon satisfied me by saying that he felt a wish to grant me a lease for fear of another day. O this word *lease!* How it entered my very heart, and caused me to bless the Lord. It is said that "the man wondering, held his peace, to wit whether the Lord had made his journey prosperous or not." Gen. xxiv.—21. And that "the man bowed down his head, and worshipped the Lord." 26v. The lease was soon made and signed. This was what I had longed for, but I could not ask my friend for it, neither did I ever give the least hint of any such desire; and he is living to witness to the truth of what I say.

I would have my reader to understand, that I never was admitted into any man's pulpit, by the wish or desire of any minister, (except at Hastings, by my worthy friend Mr. Walmsley,) neither at present do I expect it, as 'tis their wisdom to keep me out; and some have, for the present, gained much by this. It has been indirectly circulated for some years, that my distant aim is to gain a very high pulpit, or to stand in one that stands in a large and grand congregation, which is occupied by another. I have often found that what the devil is ashamed to charge the conscience with, knowing it to be false, he sets his offspring to belabour the innocent person with; and it has truly been so in this case. These persons are worse than the devil in this respect, as they have no shame: for I can truly say that I never envied any man either of his pulpit or his congregation, in part, or in the whole; and that of all the places in which I ever stood up, there is no place so valuable and so precious to me as my own; neither do I expect ever to find one; for what makes the place so dear to me is, because it has cost me many cries and groans. And Rachel said, "With great wrestlings have I wrestled with my sister, and I have prevailed: and she called his name Naphtali." Gen. xxx.—8.

In this house from love to the giver, I have performed in our low estate, the lowest services with the greatest chearfulness, and I have shed many a tear in this employment at the remembrance of the goodness of the giver.

Many a time have I gone up to this house, bowed down under many sore temptations, and tormented by the enemy's insinuating that the Lord would leave me, and would not condescend either to appear, or give me his special help; so that like the Apostle, "My flesh had no rest but I was troubled on every side; without were fightings, within were fears." 2 Cor. vii.—5. "And I was with you in weakness, and in fear, and in much trembling. And my speech and my preaching was not with enticing words of man's wisdom, but in demonstration of the spirit and of power: that your faith should not stand in the wisdom of men, but in the power of God." 1 Cor. ii.—3, 5. O how I have trembled, and in this state have begun to speak, when all on a sudden the Lord has broken in upon me with a little light, and a little dew on my spirit! O how this has chased away my enemies, and endeared the Lord of life and glory to me! O to have a feeling sense of standing in the strength of the Lord, and for his strength to be made perfect in our weakness, and our loins to be girded with his strength, and his light to shine forth on the word; how exceedingly precious it is.

There is one thing that I would not forget to mention, as it may be useful to some one that may come after in the way of tribulation: which is, that I received much help at different times from an observation that dropped from the late Mr. Huntington, full ten years before the benefit of it was felt by me; when I heard him make it, it was of no value to me, and it was the least of my thoughts that it ever would be. It was this: that he was tempted and tried during six years at every time that he finished a sermon, to draw the conclusion and believe that it was the last that he should ever deliver, and that he should have nothing to say to the people at the next time of preaching. This was brought to my remembrance, and often made of especial use to me.

Our Lord saith "Whosoever drinketh of the water that I shall give him shall never thirst; but the water that I shall give him shall be in him a well of water springing up into everlasting life." John iv.—14. And Solomon saith, that "the words of a man's mouth are as deep waters, and the well spring of wisdom as a flowing brook." Prov. xviii.—4. But I often found the water very low, and temptation very hot; and in great drought I doubted that all would be burnt up, and that famine would ensue: often when I have been drawing these conclusions the springs have suddenly begun to break and spring up; then O what a singing unto it, "Spring up, O well; sing ye unto it." Num. xxi.—17. How pleasant it is to fill the watering troughs when this is the case! "He that watereth shall be watered also himself." Prov. xi—25. At this time there is no keeping any of it back, but a pouring it forth; freely receiving and freely giving; this is the clouds emptying themselves. "If the clouds be full of rain, they empty themselves upon the earth." Eccles. xi.—3. There is no keeping back part until another time lest the clouds should return empty; nor fear of the time of drought. "Blessed is the man that trusteth in the Lord, and whose hope the Lord is. For he shall be as a tree planted by the waters, and that spreadeth out her roots by the river, and shall not see when heat cometh, but her leaf shall be green: and shall not be careful in the year of draught, neither shall cease from yielding fruit." Jer. xvii.—7, 8. Here is letting the morrow take thought for itself, and having our bread given us daily, that it may be fresh and new; which was shadowed forth under the Mosaical Dispensation by the bread that was to be placed on the golden table every sabbath day hot, when the stale was to be removed.

I have often wondered how a man can preach sabbath-day after sabbath-day, from the same text; and it is a mystery to me how a man that receives all by the spirit, can retain the life and savour of it on his spirit so long; for my own part I will publicly acknowledge that I cannot do so, and I will give my reasons for it:—

In the first place, for the most part I remain somewhat quiet in my mind till the time draws near, and then there begins to be a searching both within and without; not searching after doctrine or the letter of the word, for that in a measure, I already have in my judgment; but what I am searching for, is, a word to be given me by the blessed spirit. "The Lord gave the word. Psa. xviii.—11. Now, it is the substance of that text that I want, and when that is given me, although it may be but a small portion, yet being attended with dew or the excellency of the power, it is sufficient: "For as the rain cometh down, and the snow from heaven, and returneth not thither, but watereth the earth, and maketh it bring forth and bud, that it may give seed to the sower, and bread to the eater; so shall my word be that goeth forth out of my mouth: it shall not return unto me void, but it shall accomplish that which I please, and it shall prosper in the thing whereto I sent it." Isa. lv.—10, 11. Now this is having seed given to the sower and bread to the eater: "Jesus saith unto them, children, have ye any meat? They answered him, No. And he said unto them, cast the net on the right side of the ship, and ye shall find." John xxi.--5, 6. Now this creates nourishment that is appointed to sustain the bride's sinking spirits, and must be received fresh and new every time; for, as in a temporal sense, that which I received a day or two ago will not give me refreshing succour and strength to day, or to-morrow; so I find it to be in a spiritual sense. "It is the spirit that quickeneth; the flesh profiteth nothing; the words that I speak unto you, they are spirit, and they are life." John vi.--63. First obtain this word a fresh, then it gives freshness, and reanimation to the new man. "The husbandman that laboureth must be first partaker of the fruits." 2 Tim. ii.---6. This I find to be true; he must first partake, "That he may say to the prisoners, go forth; to them that are in darkness, shew yourselves. They shall feed in the ways, and their pastures shall be in all high places." Isa. xlix.-6. The man must first receive, then as an under shepherd he feedeth the flock. "He shall feed his flock like a shepherd: he shall gather the lambs with his arm, and carry them in his bosom, and shall gently lead those that are with young." Isa. xl.---11. "Tell me, O thou whom my soul loveth, where thou feedest, where thou makest thy flock to rest at noon: for why should I be as one that turneth aside by the flocks of thy companions?" Songs i.---7. "Save thy people, and bless thine inheritance: feed them also, and lift them up for ever." Psa. xxviii.---9. And as literally no flock will do well long on the same walk; so the Lord's sheep of his pasture need fresh pastures. They that have no changes have no filial fear. Psa. lv.--19. According to their changes, their pasture needs changing.

I know that a man may learn to preach to please carnal professors, in the same manner that a boys learns his trade, or as a scholar learns his lesson to say it by rote, or as a counsellor his brief to plead; and thus do these men by the strength of their memory gather up and retain an abundance of scripture portions and sentences or texts, and being thus furnished, and having in order of consistency the letter of the word, they can, and do preach half a score of sermons from the same text, that they may be admired for their great abilities, and verily they have their reward; and what should prevent them from doing this, seeing that their kingdom stands in word, and in the excellence of their speech, and in the strength of their understanding, which enables them to ransack the written word from beginning to end, to the blinding of the eyes of the simple and unwary; but the kingdom of God stands in power, and in righteousness, and in the joy of the Holy Ghost. Therefore the Lord will spoil all this glory, strength, and excellency of man, in his own children, that he may drive them out of confidence in the wisdom of the flesh. "And I, brethren, when I came to you, came not with excellency of speech or wisdom, declaring unto you the testimony of God. And I was with you in weakness and in fear, and in much trembling. And my speech and my preaching was not with enticing words of man's wisdom, but in demonstration of the spirit and of power: that your faith should not stand in the wisdom of men, but in the power of God." 1 Cor. ii.—1, 3, 5.

"The Lord gave the word." Psa. lxviii.—11. Now 'tis this gift, that constitutes the man able to speak a word in season to him that is weary and faint. "The Lord God hath given me the tongue of the learned, that I should know how to speak a word in season to him that is weary: he wakeneth morning by morning, he wakeneth mine ear to hear as the learned. The Lord God hath opened mine ear, and I was not rebellious, neither turned away back." Isa. l.—4, 5. This is the learning that will make a man a workman that needeth not to be ashamed, rightly dividing the law and gospel, and to preach the preaching, that the Lord bid him. Jonah iii.—2. Therefore he being divested of all his own strength and ability, is constrained, sorely against his own flesh, to wait and depend on the immediate supply of the promised spirit. "Take no thought how or what ye shall speak : for it shall be given you in that same hour what ye shall speak. For it is not ye that speak, but the spirit of your Father which speaketh in you." Matt. x. —19, 20.

I believe that some good men have slipped on this ground, that a text which may have been given to them, they have spun out so long, that although at the beginning dew and savour attended it, it has all passed away and they have become dry and without savour before they have finished. If any man can prove that it is not so, I am content that the practice should be continued. I have only shewed my opinion, "Great men are not always wise ; neither do the aged understand judgment. Therefore I said hearken to me ; I also will shew mine opinion." Job xxxii.—9, 10.

But, to return, concerning our little old Chapel : after much crying down both in public pulpits, and in private tea parties, we gradually grew, although slowly; not like a poplar tree, but more like an olive that is borne down with weight and grows slowly; in the first place it became necessary to have the partition that divided the place into two parts, taken down and removed altogether; and in time the place was so full that the heat became almost unbearable, the building being of a very low pitch; several persons applied to me to have the ceiling broken up, and placed higher, to give ease from the heat; but this I could not comply with, for two reasons; first, it was my determination never to injure my landlord's property, which this would do, as there was a loft or room over the chapel which must in such case be removed; and secondly it would cost not less than thirty or forty pounds, and when done it would give us only half the relief we wanted, as it would give us no more sitting room than we already had; and I had for years had a secret persuasion, that the time would come, when we must have more room; therefore when pressed to this alteration, I used to waive it, or turn it off as well as I could. And I can truly say that I always was careful of causing my friends to be at any expence, knowing that they were but " a feeble folk," Prov. xxx—26, and very few of them but what had suffered on account of their adherence to me; and I have the same feeling towards them to this day, and would rather take the suffering side, than that they should; knowing that my day must be short; as the Apostle saith, "the time is short; it remaineth, that both they that have wives be as though they had none; and they that weep, as though they wept not; and they that rejoice, as though they rejoiced not; and they that buy, as though they possessed not; and they that use this world, as not abusing it; for the fashion of this world passeth away." 1 Cor. vii.—29, 31.

After this had been weighed over many times by me; in the autumn of the year 1824, two fresh friends called on me with the same request of having the ceiling removed; I told them it could be of no essential benefit, as we wanted sitting room as well as easement from the heat, and therefore it would not be advisable to spend money in such an alteration, when it would answer but one purpose, and at the same time we wanted to accomplish two. Therefore I hoped that they would go home and consider it over, whether it was advisable to make the place larger or not; and if objections arose in their minds against an enlargement, all was well in my mind, and I would engage never to bring the subject up to them another day; but that if after all objections that might arise in their minds, the thoughts of enlargement should rise up above all, then they should call on me another day, and thus we parted. In the mean time I prayed the Lord that if it was not consistent with his will, that the place should be altered, that he would give me a sign of it, and the sign should be this, that these friends should find objections to it, and call on me no more. In a few days one of these friends called again and declared that he had no rest for the thoughts of the house laying in so desolate a condition and so oppressed with heat, and he therefore wished from his heart, for an enlargement, my reply was, " if it be so, I will give notice for the people to meet and consider the propriety of an alteration, and all matters shall be carried by the majority.

The meeting was accordingly called, when the necessity and propriety of enlarging the house was carried almost without opposition, and it was agreed that the place should be made nearly twice the size it then was ; and wonderful to tell, within five days after it was so settled there was, without asking any person, £105. subscribed towards the work ; I say wonderful, seeing how poor the far greater part of the people were. " In a great trial of affliction the abundance of their joy and their deep poverty abounded unto the riches of their liberality. For to their power, I bear record, yea, and beyond their power they were willing of themselves ;" 2 Cor. viii.—2, 3. And in a very short time, nearly £150. was subscribed, being within £35. of what the alteration came to. The alteration was immediately commenced, and was completed in the spring of the following year.

Some may say "what a great ado you make about so old and contemptable a place, have we not so far more grand and valuable places of worship, and yet we make no such a great ado about them?" In answer to which, I acknowledge that your houses are far more grand and noble than ours, and that you make no such boast about them as I do about ours; and I should wonder if you did, when you have seen no such footsteps of divine providence in the obtaining of them. What made the sword of Goliah so valuable to David, that he said there was none like it? Doubtless the manner in which he obtained it. And 'tis the cost of obtaining a commodity that makes it valuable; and this is the reason why you can say nothing like what I have said. How have I seen these words fulfilled, "The children which thou shalt have, after thou hast lost the other, shall say again in thine ears, the place is too strait for me: give place to me that I may dwell. Then shalt thou say in thine heart, who hath begotten me these, seeing I have lost my children, and am desolate, a captive, and removing to and fro? and who hath brought up these? Behold I was left alone; these, where had they been?" Isa. xlix.—20, 21.

It was a reigning desire of my heart, that I

might bring up my family by the work of my hands, and not be living on the labour of my friends, but that I might serve them without fee or reward: this in part, I have been enabled to do, although I have been in a very infirm state of health for several years; the four children that I had before I was called to the Ministry, I have been blessed to see settled, and the Lord has provided for them, which was according to the tenor of the agreement; and with respect to my youngest son, who was born in my master's service, I have hinted to some of my friends that it would be their bounden duty to take care of him if I should not live to see him able to get his bread; notwithstanding, after providence had provided for the four first, I wished to provide for this younger one also, which I have been enabled to do hitherto, and he being now arrived to the age of fourteen years, if no affliction befalls him my friends will have but a short time to care for him in case I should be taken away.

I have been for some years persuaded that the Lord would, in his own good time, deliver me from my daily labour, without my applying for it. The Lord knoweth how trying my labour has been these last few years in my declining age, and the infirm state of health that I have so many years laboured under; and I can truly say that I served my people with as much good will, and constant attention, and been as careful not to disappoint them, as I could have done or been if they kept or supported me; and this I did freely, without fee or reward, for about or nearly fifteen years; and should have done so longer if it had been left to my choice, and I had had strength; but when the Lord's time drew near, he put it into the hearts of some of my well-wishers to insist on my acceptance of their bounty to keep me for the future without work, as a tribute of gratitude and respect for services that were past, as well as for those that they were in hopes were to come. This was not my time for it, for that was not yet come, and I gave them my reasons for it; but that availed nothing, for the most part were come to a fixed determination that it should be so, therefore I yielded to their wishes with this declaration, that I would not ask any person to sanction their views nor plans; and I have stood to my promise, for I have not gone to any person, to say, Why do you not do so? or, I wish you to do so; or, 'tis your duty to do so after the many years that I have served you; and I believe that I never shall: for I believe that the Lord's time is come, and that he will reward me, and pay me to the full for all that I have suffered for his name's sake, in labour, in reproach, in persecution, and in necessity: for the promise is, "Them that honour me I will honour;" and "Verily there is a reward." "Behold his reward is with him, and his work before him." Isa. xl.—10. And I hope that my enemies will patiently and quietly look on, and wait the result, as I am before their eyes; and their time to shout will be when the Lord leaves me both in his light and in his truth, in his providence and in his grace, and not till then; for the promise is, "The hand of the Lord shall be known towards his servants, and his indignation towards his enemies. For, behold, the Lord will come with fire, and with his chariots like a whirlwind, to render his anger with fury, and his rebuke with flames of fire. For by fire and by his sword will the Lord plead with all flesh: and the slain of the Lord shall be many." Isa. lxvi.—14, 16. And surely I have seen much of this promise fulfilled already, and I believe that I shall see more of it accomplished: not that I am the man that makes a boast, or that triumphs at the sight of judgments, far be that from me, for I can truly say with the psalmist, "My flesh trembleth for fear of thee; and I am afraid of thy judgments." Psa. cix.—120. And if he was so to deal with me, he would be perfectly just, for I am constrained to say, as the church said, "It is of the Lord's mercies that we are not consumed, because his compassions fail not." Lam. iii.—22. and as David said in one of his troubles, "If he thus say, I have no delight in thee: behold, here am I, let him do to me as seemeth good unto him." 2. Sam. xv.—26.

The Lord has often warned me of trouble, and dangers, and enemies, and likewise foretold me of joy and good, by dreams; and I have often found that "God speaketh once, yea twice, yet man perceiveth it not. In a dream, in a vision of the night, when deep sleep falleth upon men, in slumberings upon their beds; then he openeth the ears of men, and sealeth their instruction." Job. xxx.—14, 16. But many a vain and light professor in this declining day makes a scoff at such things: I know that there are many dreams which come through the multitude of business; and that many a vain and filthy obscenity is presented to the mind by the enemy, who often draws the mind through such horrid scenes that the bare recollection thereof makes the modest person blush, although no one but himself is privy to it; and I can say with sorrow, that I have often gone to bed in much sweetness and sense of peace, and awoke in the morning in guilt and gloom and great heaviness, entirely on account of the enemy dragging me in the regions of imagination through all that is detestable and most to be abhorred. But shall we cast away treasure, because it is found where filth and defilement often are? God forbid. Suppose that the patriarchs had done so, what a loss would they have sustained; and they had as much reason to do so as you or I, for they were men of like passions with you and me, they had no more holiness in their flesh than you or I have; for in their flesh dwelt no good thing; and I am certain that in their flesh dwelt as much evil, as there does in you or me; if there did not, why did they groan and cry out under their burden and wait to be delivered from it. Rom. viii.—23. I do believe that the Lord often speaks to his own in a dream, which you may see in Jer. xxiii.—28. Gen. xxxi.—11, 13, and xxxvii.—5. Matt. i.—20. and in Acts ii.—17.

I often find that the dream which comes from the Lord, whether for a warning of some evil, or for a token of good, and however I may have been inclined to put it away or turn a deaf ear to it, has presented itself to my mind, and sounded again and again; and I believe, that more or less it will always be the case; I shall mention but one, although I have had many, that I consider to be sacred as coming immediately from the Lord: for he speaketh once, yea twice in a vision or dream of the night. The dream that I shall relate, I had, when I was about fourteen or fifteen years of age, before I had any knowledge either of the Lord or of the way to be saved.

I dreamed that I was in a desert or wilderness, such as I never saw with my bodily eyes; ("He found him in a desert land, and in the waste howling wilderness." Deut. xxxii.—10.) in this wilderness there appeared no path, but all was overgroan with thickets; and like the land of

Israel in the days of Shamgar, when "the highways were unoccupied, and the travellers walked through byways, and the inhabitants of the villages ceased, they ceased in Israel." Judges v.—6, 7. In this wilderness I wandered many a weary step, with a heart full of trouble, often so entangled that I caught many a fall; and as there was no person to be seen, nor the foot-print of any, I concluded that no one ever passed through the place before: but it appeared to be "a land of deserts and of pits, a land of drought, and of the shadow of death, a land that no man passed through, and where no man dwelt." Jer. ii.—6. After much wearisomeness and fainting I came to a large gulf, that appeared to be impassible, and to extend to the uttermost extremity of the earth, on the north and south, so that it was utterly impossible for me either to see or find either end of it; and as I was standing on the western brink of it, a voice said to me, you must pass through to the opposite shore, I "heard the voice of the words, but saw no similitude." Deut. iv.—12. O how my heart sunk at the sound of the words, and the sight of that which was before me! The gulf did not appear to be water, but as mud after water has been drained off it. The appearance of it is as perfect in my mind to this day as it was then. After I had stood a long time hesitating and trembling on the brink, an unseen power caught hold of me, and cast me into the bog; Mr. Hart says

"Oh! the pangs by Christians felt,
  When their eyes are open;
When they see the gulphs of guilt
  They must wade and grope in;"

And so I found it in my dream. I waded here in this helpless case a long time, and concluded that I must be smothered, as I sunk so deep in this mud that it entered my mouth; as it began thus to enter, my breath shortened, and I concluded that I should sink to rise no more: when just as I was sinking below the surface, and in answer to my sighs for deliverance, an unseen power was felt, that raised me from this sinking state and brought me to the opposite shore, which was on the eastern side of the gulf; and there appeared another insurmountable difficulty, as the shore was so lofty and high, and moreover, though the western shore came sloping down to the gulf, yet this side was perpendicular, like a great cliff; in a moment, an unseen power wafted me to the summit with as much ease, as though I had been divested of all the gross matter of the mortal body; and as it will be when this corruptible, shall have put on incorruption, and this mortal have put on immortality. 1 Cor. xv.—53. As soon as I found a firm standing on the summit, I cast my eyes toward the north, from which the path lay sloping downwards towards me; and as I ascended towards it, such glory, and shining lustre appeared before me, as I never saw with my natural eyes. It shone and appeared like a city; but the glory of the shining of the inhabitants, and of the pavement thereof surpassed all that mortal man can describe, the lustre was so great that I have no language sufficient, no, nor ever shall, to set it forth. In the twinkling of an eye it was wispered to me, " This is to be your residence;" at this I blushed, and said can that be possible, seeing that I am naked and all over besmeared with the filthy mud of that gulf that I have just waded through; on saying this, I was directed to look from the glory of the city (for so I call it, to convey if possible, the clear view I had of it in some measure to you) down on myself, I accordingly looked from the glory of the place down on my own person, when the view of myself astonished me as much as the glory that I was going towards; for I expected to have seen myself covered all over with filth and mud, and naked; but to my great wonder and astonishment, not a particle of the filth that I had so lately been covered with remained on me, nor the least particle of any of the effects of it; but I was as pure and glorious as the city, the pavement, or the inhabitants that I saw; and as full of raptures of joy as I could hold, and thought that I should burst out in shouts of joy; and really did, so as to cause myself to awake; when to my sorrow, I found it to be only a dream.

"They shall call them, the holy people, the redeemed of the Lord: and thou shalt be called, Sought out, a city not forsaken." Isa. lxii.—12. "Glorious things are spoken of thee, O city of God." Psa. lxxxvii.—3. "And he carried me away in the spirit to a great and high mountain, and shewed me that great city, the holy Jerusalem, descending out of heaven from God, having the glory of God: and her light was like unto a stone most precious, even like a jasper stone, clear as crystal." Rev. xxi.—10, 11. "And the street of the city was pure gold, as it were transparent glass. And I saw no temple therein; for the Lord God Almighty and the Lamb are the temple of it. And the city had no need of the Sun, neither of the Moon, to shine in it: for the glory of God did lighten it, and the Lamb is the light thereof. And the nations of them which are saved shall walk in the light of it: and the kings of the earth do bring their glory and honour into it." 21, 24v.

Now reader, I have related to you this dream in simplicity, and can affirm what I have said to be truth, and you have my consent to put whatever construction upon it you please; as for myself, I believe I have seen part of it fulfilled already, and the whole in the Lord's time I doubt not will be also fulfilled. One thing that I would not omit is, what I have been astonished at:—that although I had this dream in the early part of my life, yet I lost the very recollection of it until after the Lord delivered me from "so great a death," 2 Cor. i.—10. when it was brought to my recollection as fresh and perfect as it was when I first received it: and I often lose sight and remembrance of it for a long time, even to this day; and it often surprises me that it should be so, but so it is, this is the truth and nothing but the truth.

But my reader may be desirous of hearing of some of my temptations: as for them, either from some quarter or other I have seldom been free, either within or without; and am oftentimes so beset by the workings of sin in my flesh, that I have reason to complain with the psalmist, that "my life is spent with grief, and my years with sighing: my strength faileth because of mine iniquity, and my bones are consumed." Psa. xxxi.—10. But for you or me to expect any man to shew us all his temptations, is to expect what will never be realised; for I believe that all men, more or less, have a portion of modesty or decency belonging to them. But if a man of God was to shew all the workings of evil that he is exercised with, he could have but little of either modesty or decency. Even the Apostle does not speak out to the full, but leaves this for you and me to conjecture: all that he says is, " there was given to me a thorn in the flesh." 2 Cor. xii.--7. And another says, " I hate vain thoughts." Psa. cxix,—113. And another says, "Surely I am more brutish than any man."

Prov. xxx.—2. And another says, "The heart is deceitful above all things, and desperately wicked: who can know it?" Jer. xvii.—9. And another says, "O wretched man that I am! Who shall deliver me from the body of this death?" Rom. vii.—24. And the poet says

> "Deep quagmires choak the way!
> Corruptions foul and thick;
> Whose stench infects the air, and makes
> The strongest trav'ler sick."

And you ought not to wish any man to make himself, in the eyes of men that are strangers to the evil of their hearts and to the temptations of the devil, a butt for laughter. Therefore I shall beg to be excused. But if any one has a desire for the easing of their own minds; as there are but few, I am persuaded, if any, but what are labouring under some sore temptation, and for the most part concluding that theirs is a singular one; in which conclusion I believe they are very wrong. I say, if any one of these should wish to know mine, let them call on me in private. remembering this word, "The same afflictions are accomplished in your brethren that are in the world." 1 Peter v.--9. And that "the tongue of the wise useth knowledge aright." Prov. xv. —2. "He that hath knowledge spareth his words." 17, and 27v.

The Lord having been pleased to keep me very low, for the most part, in the things of this world, I have found the enemy take great advantage of me, on the substance of this text, "Seek ye not what ye shall eat, or what ye shall drink, neither be ye of doubtful mind. For all these things do the nations of the world seek after: and your Father knoweth that ye have need of these things." Luke xii.—29, 30. In the day when all my family was at home, and my friends were forsaking me, and turning to be my enemies, what hours of conflict I had with the enemy, who was always pointing me to the things that were seen, and the great hazard that I was exposing my family to, so that I could often say as Naomi did, " It grieveth me much for your sakes, that the hand of the Lord is gone out against me." Ruth i.—13. How often I strove to have my own way, but I found this to be true, "He is of one mind, and who can turn him? And what his soul desireth, even that he doeth." Job xxii—13. And this in Hosea "I will hedge up thy way with thorns, and make a wall, that she shall not find her paths." ii.—6. A word to the wise, I trust is sufficient to take my meaning without any further explanation.

I have been much tried in my time on this portion of Holy Writ, " Whosoever drinketh of the water that I shall give him shall never thirst." John iv.—14. I have heard men declare the meaning of it was: that whoever drinks of this water never desires any of the enjoyments of this present world, but becomes so sanctified and so dead to this world, that the whole has lost its charms and has no attraction for him. Being but a child in understanding, in times past I was much tossed in my mind respecting this: for when the Lord first appeared to me and spoke peace to my soul, and all the while that peace and joy lasted with me in the life and glory of it; I felt no motions of lust; but was free, not only from the guilt of sin, but from the feelings and motions of it also; and was risen above the whole: but when my beloved withdrew himself, I returned to my own place, and found a principle within, that surprised me, "For the good that I would I do not: but the evil which I would not, that I do. I find then a law, that, when I would do good, evil is present with me. And I see a law in my members, warring against the law of my mind, and bringing me into captivity to the law of sin which is in my members." Rom. vii.--19, 21, 23. Hereupon I was sure that all was not right, either what I heard men declare was wrong, or I was wrong; for I felt a principle within me that loved sin; or a sensual appetite that lusted or desired for gratification.

I was tossed about here until the spirit opened my eyes to see the two nations, or the two armies within me; Songs vi.---13. or the flesh and the spirit, and to understand that the flesh of a man of God who had the spirit of life, was no better than that of a stranger to God, but worse; "For they are not in trouble as other men; neither are they plagued like other men. Therefore pride compasseth them about as a chain;" Psa. lxxiii.---5, 6. and the lamentation of the spouse suited me, " I am black, as the tents of Kedar." Songs i.---5. " Woe is me, that I sojourn in Meshech, that I dwell in the tents of Kedar!" Psa. cxx.---5. The flesh struggles the more desperately for being nailed to the Cross. "Our old man is crucified with Christ, that the body of sin might be destroyed, that henceforth we should not serve sin." Rom. vi.---6.

The meaning of the text I apprehend to be this; when God the Father chastens a son out of his law, the feelings are set forth under the idea of the tongue failing for thirst; " when the poor and needy seek water, and there is none, and their tongues faileth for thirst, I the Lord will hear them," Isa. xli.—17, and in Isaiah, xxxv.—7, it is said, that " the parched ground shall become a pool, and the thirsty land springs of water:" here we have *parched* and *failing for thirst,* holding forth the fire that scorches the sinner; " from his right hand went a fiery law for them." Deut. xxxiii.—2. This fire causes an intense heat, so that it made the Psalmist say, " day and night thy hand was heavy upon me: my moisture is turned into the drought of summer." Psa. xxxii.—4. This awakening is thus set forth by this similitude; and sure I am, that 'tis like drought and parching heat. And the manifestation of an interest in the Lord Jesus, is set forth under the similitude of drinking of water or wine, "give strong drink unto him that is ready to perish, and wine unto those that be of heavy hearts. Let him drink, and forget his poverty, and remember his misery no more." Prov. xxxi.—6, 7. "As cold water is to a thirsty soul, so is good news from a far country." Prov. xxv.—25. "They shall be abundantly satisfied with the fatness of thy house; and thou shalt make them drink of the river of thy pleasures." Psa. xxxvi.—8. "They did all drink the same spiritual drink: for they drank of that spiritual rock that followed them, and that rock was Christ." 1 Cor. x.—4. The first drop of which is sufficient to remove all the feeling sense of the revelation of God's wrath or anger, or the heat or fire that is revealed by the law; and by this the thirst is allayed: and whatever may be the temptations or bereavements, doubt or darkness that we may be subject to, no more of that anger or intense heat will ever be felt by us, to cause such a thirst as has been felt by us before; "There is a river, the streams whereof shall make glad the city of God, the holy place of the tabernacles of the most high." Pas. xlvi.—4. And the love and kindness of God our Saviour is set forth under the similitude of a cold flowing brook, and the sinner under the similitude of a chased hart. "As the hart panteth after the water brooks, so panteth my soul after thee, O God. My soul thirsteth for God, for the living God: when shall I come and appear before God?" Psa. xlii.—1, 2. Remember reader, that the same misery is to be found no more. I have proved in this matter also, that none teacheth like God; for he teacheth to profit.

I have in times past been much perplexed about the law, and for several years was greatly tried between men's different opinions respecting it; which made me beg of the Lord to shew me what was right, before he would suffer me to hold it forth in public; lest I should preach the opinion of any man, and afterwards have to see my error therein: therefore I was silent on so weighty a point, until the Lord opened my understanding in this matter; and since that I have not been shy or ashamed to declare my belief.

My perplexity arose from this cause; many declared that the law was not to be preached, except only as the rule of a believer's conduct; and that it had nothing to do in the awakening or alarming of a sinner: all that was to be preached, was, what they called Gospel, or the unconditional promises, or God's gracious love and favour in the gift of his only begotten son. These sentiments I knew to be wrong; " to the law and to the testimony: if they speak not according to this word, it is because there is no light in them." Isa. viii.—20. And this word saith "Blessed is the man whom thou chastenest, O Lord, and teachest him out of thy law." Psa. xciv.—12. "Think not that I am come to destroy the law, or the prophets : I am not come to destroy, but to fulfil." Matt. v.—17. " It is written in the prophets, and they shall be all taught of God. Every man therefore that hath heard, and hath learned of the father, cometh unto me." John vi.--45, and the Apostle affirms, that the law is our schoolmaster, " wherefore the law was our schoolmaster unto Christ, that we might be justified by faith. But after that faith is come, we are no longer under a schoolmaster." Gal. iii.—24, 25, " What shall we say then? Is the law sin? God forbid. Nay, I had not known sin, but by the law : for I had not known lust, except the law had said, thou shalt not covet. But sin, taking occasion by the commandment, wrought in me all manner of concupiscence. For without the law sin was dead. For I was alive without the law once : but when the commandment came, sin revived, and I died. And the commandment, which was ordained to life, I found to be unto death. For sin, taking occasion by the commandment, deceived me, and by it slew me." Rom. vii.— 7, 11. "Now we know that what things soever the law saith, it saith to them who are under the law : that every mouth may be stopped, and all the world may become guilty before God. Therefore by the deeds of the law there shall no flesh be justified in his sight: for by the law is the knowledge of sin." Rom. iii.—19, 20.

Now as many as God sets his love upon before time, he rebukes and chastens; and these find that the law is a severe schoolmaster: the man that has never been at this school, cannot know what a sinner he is, for this is to give this knowledge: "by the law is the knowledge of sin," and when it enters, it will cause sin to revive, of which the man had no knowledge before; it "wrought in me all manner of concupiscence." "Moreover the law entered, that the offence might abound." Rom. v.—20, and wherever it enters, sin will abound.

The person that has escaped the scourges and lashings of this schoolmaster knows of nothing more than outward sin and trangression, and knows nothing of the spirituality of the law that apprehends for the thoughts, lusts, and motions that are within, in the secret recesses of the heart; for until this plough enters there is no discovery of these things; but when it enters, the secrets of the heart, which are evil and that continually, are made manifest; and the impossibility of ceasing from evil, and of doing good, is known and painfully felt: till at length the sinner is brought in this way even unto death: and except a corn of wheat drop into the earth and die, it abides alone: here all flesh comes in guilty and every mouth is stopped: and until this is the case, the natural hope of man will never be cut off nor perish. "The axe is laid unto the root of the trees: every tree therefore which bringeth not forth good fruit is hewn down, and cast into the fire." Luke iii.—9. But "there is hope of a tree, if it be cut down, that it will sprout again, and that the tender branch thereof will not cease." Job xiv.—7. "He maketh sore, and bindeth up: he woundeth, and his hands make whole." Job v.—18. "Thine arrows stick fast in me," (saith the psalmist) "and thy hand presseth me sore." Psa. xxxviii.—2. And Paul saith "knowing therefore the terror of the Lord, we persuade men." 2 Cor. v. 11. And the Psalmist also saith, "I am afflicted and ready to die from my youth up: while I suffer thy terrors I am distracted. Thy fierce wrath goeth over me; thy terrors have cut me off." Psa. lxxxviii—15, 16. And our Lord saith "Ye shall indeed drink of the cup that I drink of." And if my reader should live and die a stranger to this, he can never say with the church, "remembering mine affliction and my misery, the wormwood and the gall. My soul hath them still in remembrance, and is humbled in me. This I recall to my mind, therefore have I hope." Lam. iii.—19, 21. Neither this in Isaiah "And in that day thou shalt say, O Lord I will praise thee: though thou wast angry with me, thine anger is turned away, and thou comfortedst me." xii.—1.

These are some of the lessons that we learn by this schoolmaster; and this is preaching the law lawfully; and "we know that the law is good, if a man use it lawfully, 1 Tim. i.—8, and this is establishing the law. Rom. iii.—31. "For whom the Lord loveth he chasteneth, and scourgeth every son whom he receiveth. If ye endure chastening, God dealeth with you as with sons; for what son is he whom the father chasteneth not? But if ye be without chastisement, whereof all [sons] are partakers, then are ye bastards, and not sons." Heb. xii.—6, 8. And if this be not the case with you, whatever claim you may have on the Lord, ye are but bastards. Remember you have been warned of the evil consequence of departing this life without a feeling sense of this teaching of the Father. You may say, "we have eaten and drank in thy presence, and cast out devils, and done many wonderful works;" but he will not ratify your claim on him, but will disannul your arrogant and presumptuous pretences, by saying I never knew you; depart from me ye workers of iniquity. And I am appointed to tell you in time that ye are nothing but bastards; for if ye are without chastisement, whereof all his children are partakers, then are ye bastards, and not sons.

Every man that shall enter the holy city, shall in time, sing this song, "I will sing of mercy and judgment: unto thee, O Lord, will I sing"

Psa. ci.—1; of judgment past, and mercy come; for "judgment shall return unto righteousness: and all the upright in heart shall follow it." Psa. xciv.—15. I would ask you what sort of a song you expect to sing. I read that the Law came by Moses, and Grace and Truth by Jesus Christ: and the soul when disburthened of this mortality will be carried into ultimate glory, where the song that was so imperfectly learnt and sung here, shall be perfected. "When that which is perfect is come, then that which is in part shall be done away." 1 Cor. xiii.—10. "And there they sing the song of Moses the servant of God, and the song of the Lamb." Rev. xv,—3.

Some one will say, if this be the entrance of the way, I have not stepped one step in it yet. I answer, this certainly is the way, and the right way "to a city of habitation." Psa. cvii.—7. For "we must through much tribulation enter into the kingdom of God." Acts xiv.—22. You may see the beginning and end of your race thus set forth in Ezekiel. xlvi.—9. "When the people of the land shall come before the Lord in the solemn feasts, he that entereth in by the way of the north gate to worship, shall go out by the way of the south gate; and he that entereth by the way of the south gate shall go forth by the way of the north gate; he shall not return by the way of the gate whereby he came in, but shall go forth over against it." The entering by the south, signifies the receiving of the word with joy; or what is commonly called by unlearned men, being drawn by love, or coming by an easy way; these being never taught by the spirit, for where he comes he convinces of sin. John xvi.—8. This easy path is thus set forth by the south door. But the north door holds forth our being brought to pass under the rod. "I will cause you to pass under the rod; and I will bring you into the bond of the covenant." Ezek. xx.—37. If God has called you by his grace, and revealed his dear son in you, you have at the entrance found this portion of holy writ verified: "I will be unto Ephraim as a Lion, and as a young Lion to the house of Judah: I, even I, will tear and go away; I will take away, and none shall rescue him. I will go and return to my place, till they acknowledge their offence, and seek my face: in their affliction they will seek me early." Hosea v.—14, 15. And this also, "the voice of the Lord shaketh the wilderness; the Lord shaketh the wilderness of Kadesh. The voice of the Lord maketh the hinds to calve, and discovereth the forests." Psa. xxix.—8, 9. And just as you felt in your awakenings, so will these easy path men and carnal professors feel when God calls them to leave this world and to appear before him: then will they begin to call on the rocks and mountains to hide them from him that sets upon the throne.

I have no doubt but that some will rebel and

fight against this truth, and belabour me, both in the pulpit, and at their feasts and tea parties, and draw me in all manner of frightful shapes and figures: but two things I will tell you:—first, you cannot make me appear in a worse light then I have seen myself in: for I have had the mystery of iniquity opened up to me, and therefore I defy any man to blacken me with a deeper dye: and I am constrained to cry out that, in my flesh, I am black. The next thing is, if you fight against, oppose, despise, and trample this under foot, and declare that 'tis not the truth, but that there is another way to life, much easier, and that I lie, and that you will not regard my words; I will answer you in this matter as Micaiah did Zedekiah; " behold thou shalt see in that day, when thou shalt go into an inner chamber to hide thyself." 1 Kings xxii.—25. Remember that 'tis not my word, therefore beware that you cast it not behind you. For our Lord saith to his servants, " it is not ye that speak, but the spirit of your father which speaketh in you." Matt. x.—20. " And whatsoever thou shalt bind on earth, shall be bound in heaven; and whatsoever thou shalt loose on earth, shall be loosed in heaven." Matt. xvi.—19.

Many that spurn against the coming to and being chastened by the father out of his law, will contend that this law is to be their rule of life. To them I believe it is a rule of life, and ought be considered so, and to all others that have not been delivered from the curse and condemnation of it: but for them to insist that it ought to be held as a rule of life to those that have been brought to death under it, and delivered from the killing sentence of it; is an heresy that I will oppose by the Lord's help. To the free born children 'tis nothing more than a dead letter; but to the bond children, whose mother is Hagar or Mount Sinai that genders to bondage, and who are born after the flesh, it is a rule of life and a killing sentence: such as these always did, and always will persecute those that are born of the free woman, or of the spirit; and these bond children desire to be teachers of the law, understanding neither what they say, nor whereof they affirm.

It has often surprised me that the very men who are the advocates for the law being the rule of a believer's life, are those that live in the open breach of the letter of the law daily. Does not the law forbid a man to covet any thing that is his neighbour's: and can any one of these say, that they do not wish or desire at any time to have or possess something that his neighbour possesses; which is a breach of the law. Another breach is notorious; the law says, thou shalt not bear false witness against thy neighbour: which command these men also live in the breach of; for as soon as any man insists on the necessity of a deliverence from curse and condemnation by the sprinkling of the blood of Jesus, and of a deliverance from the law in its penalty and commanding rule; these men begin to rail, and with falsehood misrepresent, and with the tongue of slander speak many an untruth, on purpose to prejudice the simple." Deliver my soul, O Lord, from lying lips, and from a deceitful tongue. What shall be given unto thee? Or what shall be done unto thee, thou false tongue? Sharp arrows of the mighty with coals of Juniper." Psa. cxx.--2, 5. Another breach these men are guilty of, is in not keeping the sabbath day; they profess openly to observe the first day of the week, whilst the law says, "the seventh day is the sabbath." Exod.. xx.—10. "Six days thou shalt work, but on the seventh day thou shalt rest." Exod. xxxiv.—21. "From even unto even, shall ye celebrate your sabbath." Levit. xxiii.----32. Here we see that these law-men go point blank against the law's commands; both as to the day, and to the time of beginning it: the law says the seventh day, and to begin in the evening, and end the next evening; and the Apostle says, "what things soever the law saith, it saith to them who are under the law." Rom. iii.—19. And if they have never been deli— by the law-fulfiller, they are under its co— and curses to this day: but whom the — free, he is free indeed.

All these advocates for the —

of life to the believer, have either taken up this notion from the opinions of other men, who have been such leaders as are described in Isaiah, "as for my people, children are their oppressors, and women rule over them. O my people, they which lead thee cause thee to err, and destroy the way of thy paths." Isa. iii.—12. Or have known no more than the Apostle did before his call when he thought he was, "as touching the righteousness which is in the law blameless." Phil. iii.—6. When he knew no more than the letter of the law, which condemns outward faults; and in that respect no man could charge the Apostle with breaking the sabbath as to the outward observance of it; neither with theft, nor murder, nor of committing adultery, nor with disrespect to his parents, nor of bearing false witness against his neighbour. His conduct would bear the scrutiny of all this; and so would mine, before the Lord brought me under this schoolmaster. I greatly doubt whether many of these pleaders for the law could stand this test of the letter.

But the law will be found by God's chosen people to be spiritual, and to require holiness within. "Behold, thou desirest truth in the inward parts:" Psa. li.—6. our Lord says, that he that looketh on a woman and feels the least lust arise within, hath committed adultery with her already in his heart. Matt. v.—28. And " whosoever is angry with his brother without a cause shall be in danger of the judgment:" Matt. v.--22. and John saith "Whosoever hateth his brother is a murderer:" 1 John iii.--15. And the Apostle says that covetousness is idolatry. Col. iii.--5. And the Law saith "remember the Sabbath-day, to keep it holy," Exod. xx.---8. which is required not only in the outward shew, but in the thoughts; and the Lord says that the thoughts of man's heart is evil, and that continually; then where is the person that can stand clear, "for whosoever shall keep the whole law, and yet offend in one point, he is guilty of all." Jam. ii---10, And whatsoever the law saith, it saith to them who are under the law. Rom. iii.—19. Now this is their rule, as they are under it, and have never been delivered from the curse, " for as many as are of the works of the law are under the curse:" Gal. iii---10. nor from the penalty of it, which is eternal death. But they are not satisfied with abiding here themselves, but endeavour to have us bound and circumcised also. Acts xv.--24. Now what the law saith, it saith to them that are under it; "but now [in this present moment] we are, [and ever shall be,] delivered from the law, that being dead wherein we were held." Rom. vii.—6. And the Apostle saith, " know ye not, brethren, (for I speak to them that know the law,)" but no man knoweth the law, until the spirituality of it is made known to him, and it enters into him, then hidden sins start up or revive, and he is brought to death; then the Apostle goes on with saying, "how that the law hath dominion over a man as long as he liveth?" And as these letter-men and law-men have never died, they have a right to take it for their rule: "for the woman which hath an husband is bound by the law to her husband so long as he liveth; but if the husband be dead, she is loosed from his commanding rule, and is free to marry another man. Wherefore my brethren, ye are also become dead to the law by the body of Christ; that ye should be married to another, even to him that is raised from the dead." Rom. vii.—1, 4. For sin and law have now reigned to death; and this is coming to the end of the law, when the condemning sentence of the law brings the man to fall down and confess that God is just in condemning him, and clear in his judgment; and he falls where he concludes that he is without God and without hope in this world. This is coming to death: and the law has the command over the man till this is the case; and here the law ends. "For I through the law am dead to the law, that I might live unto God." Gal. ii.—19. "For we are dead, and our life is hid with Christ in God." Col. iii.—3. "That as sin hath reigned unto death, even so might grace reign through righteousness unto eternal life by Jesus Christ our Lord." Rom. v.—21.

Here is coming to death; and to the penalty of the law, which is death: and then comes the time of the Father's appointment: and then comes justifying faith (which is the gift of God) to lay hold of the Goodness, Mercy, and Kindness of God in his own dear Son, and power to lay hold on eternal life. This is passing from death to life, and this man is not to come again into condemnation. John v.---24. Therefore we are buried with him by baptism into death; that like as Christ was raised up from the dead by the glory of the father, even so we also should walk in newness of life. Rom. vi.---4. And " now we are delivered from the law, that being dead wherein we were held; that we should serve in newness of spirit, and not in the oldness of the letter." Rom. vii.---6. "For sin shall not have dominion over you; for ye are not under the law, but under grace. What then? Shall we sin, because we are not under the law, but under grace? God forbid." Rom. vi.---14, 15.

Here is coming under the rule and reign of God's free favour, which is said to be better than life itself, " because thy loving kindness is better than life, my lips shall praise thee." Psa. lxiii.---3. Here we become dead to the law, and the law becomes dead to us; and the nearest kinsman raises up seed, " who is made unto us wisdom, and righteousness, and sanctification, and redemption." 1 Cor. i.---30. " As a young man marrieth a virgin, so shall thy sons marry thee: and as the bridegroom rejoiceth over the bride, so shall thy God rejoice over thee." Isa. lxii.---5. "Thy maker is thine husband; the Lord of hosts is his name; and thy redeemer the holy one of Israel; the God of the whole earth shall he be called." Isa. liv.---5. " He that is joined unto the Lord is one spirit." 1 Cor. vi.---17. " For this cause shall a man leave his father and mother, and shall be joined unto his wife, and they two shall be one flesh. This is a great mystery; but I speak concerning Christ and the Church." Eph. v.---31, 32.

This Union, which existed before time began, is now made known to us; "Thus saith the Lord; I remember thee, the kindness of thy youth, the love of thine espousals, when thou wentest after me in the wilderness, in a land that was not sown." Jer. ii.—2. "Go forth, O ye daughters of Zion, and behold king Solomon with the crown wherewith his mother crowned him in the day of his espousals, and in the day of the gladness of his heart." Songs iii.—11. " My beloved is mine, and I am his: he feedeth among the lilies." Songs ii.—16.

This is being married to the Lord Christ, or entering into the bond of the covenant manifestly; and this bond is love; and the love that existed before time in God, is shed abroad in the heart by the Holy Ghost: and Oh! what a giving and taking, to have and to hold, for better and for worse, here is in the nuptial day, that can never fully be forgotten. " Can a maid forget her ornaments, or a bride her attire?" Jer. ii. 32. In that day, what a sweetness in the transfer that takes place; all my sins, past, present, and future, were imputed to him, and now I enjoy the blessing in part; and all his righteousness and sanctification is imputed and set down to my account. Here the Father is well pleased, and the bridegroom is well pleased, and the worthless bride is well pleased also. The Father declares that he is well pleased; "The Lord is well pleased for his righteousness sake." Isa. xlii —21. "This is my bloved Son, in whom I am well pleased." Matt. iii.—17. And the bridegroom declares of his Father "I do always those things that please him." John viii.—29. And of his bride "thou art all fair, my love; there is no spot in thee." Songs iv.—7. He gave himself for the church, "That he might present it to himself a glorious church, not having spot, or wrinkle, or any such thing; but that it should be holy and without blemish." Eph. v.—27. This bride is never to be viewed but only as she stands in her husband, who represents her in himself. And he prays his Father "That they may be one, as thou; Father, art in me, and I in thee, that they also may be one in us; that the world may believe that thou hast sent me. And the glory which thou gavest me I have given them; that they may be one, even as we are one: I in them, and thou in me, that they may be made perfect in one; and that the world may know that thou hast sent me, and hast loved them, as thou hast loved me." John xvii.--21, 23. Now as all mine become his and he has saved me from my sins, and purged me from dead works; "For if the blood of bulls and of goats, and the ashes of an heifer sprinkling the unclean, sanctifieth to the purifying of the flesh: how much more shall the blood of Christ, who through the eternal Spirit offered himself without spot to God, purge your conscience from dead works to serve the living God." Heb. ix.---13, 14. "And we have seen and do testify that the Father sent the Son to be the Saviour of the World." 1 John iv.---14. So all his become mine; is not this an unspeakable gift? And this is the happy lot of all that are delivered from the law and joined to this bridegroom; and "The fruit of the spirit is love, joy, peace, longsuffering, gentleness, goodness, faith, meekness, temperance; against such there is no law." Gal. v.---22, 23.

And moreover the law cannot require more than the husband has paid or rendered to it. "The Lord is well pleased for his righteousness sake; he will magnify the law and make it honourable." Isa, xlii,---21. The law has not now to do with the bride, but with the husband; if the law requires righteousness, there it is; if it requires sanctification, love, or holiness, there it is. The law has lost its commanding authority over me, for I am, as it were, wrapped in his skirt, and have nothing more to do with

Moses in my conscience, nor he with me; for he is no more than a servant, and on this mount he yields up his authority to his Lord. This is being brought into the kingdom of God's grace and favour, where I am to serve him in newness of life, having received the blessing which is life for evermore, "For there the Lord commanded the blessing, even life for evermore." Psalms cxxxiii.---3.

Perhaps my reader may be ready to ask me whether I then am lawless, and live as my flesh lists; I answer, No, by no means. How shall we that are dead to sin live in the known practice of sin? Shall we sin that grace may abound? God forbid. Our obedience flows from the newness of life. "This shall be the covenant that I will make with the house of Irsael; after those days saith the Lord, I will put my law in their inward parts, and write it in their hearts; and will be their God, and they shall be my people." Jer. xxxi.---33. Here God says he will put his law in their hearts, and he also says, "they shall be my people, and I will be their God; and I will give them one heart, and one way, that they may fear me for ever, for the good of them, and of their children after them; and I will make an everlasting covenant with them, that I will not turn away from them, to do them good; but I will put my fear in their hearts, that they shall not depart from me." Jer. xxxii.--38, 40. Here we see the Lord engages to plant his fear in their hearts, that shall last there for ever; and Paul says that he is not without the law to Christ. Now what law is this? Seeing we are delivered from the ceremonial and moral law? I answer, "The law of kindness." Prov. xxxi.---26. The wisdom that is spoken of in the Proverbs, is none less than the Lord Christ; and this is his law that is called the law of kindness. Titus iii.---4. When this appears or comes in sight, what a constraining there is. The Apostle says "the love of Christ constraineth me." The word, Law, signifies obligation. Can there be any thing to equal the undeserved love and kindness shewed to us? What great obligation this brings us under: "Her sins which are many, are forgiven; for she loved much: but to whom little is forgiven, the same loveth little." Luke vii.---47. "The law of the wise" is said to be "a fountain of life, to depart from the snares of death." Prov. xiii.---14. And the isles are said to wait for this law. Isa. xlii.---4. And James gives its full purport, and calls it the perfect law of liberty. Jas. i.--25, and ii--12. And Paul also speaks of this law when he asks, "Where is boasting then? It is excluded. By what law? Of works? Nay: but by the law of faith." Rom. iii.---27. "For" he says, "the law of the spirit of life in Christ Jesus hath made me free from the law of sin and death." Rom. viii.--2. Wherever this law is implanted it binds the soul in love and gratitude, to the giver, and the receiver can never, according to his own feelings, do enough in gratitude for the honour of his bountiful benefactor.

You may ask, how is he taught this? I answer not by the moral law, for he is by the spirit manifestly made free from that, for whom the son maketh free he is free indeed. I will tell you the fountain from whence springs and flows all service in the newness of the spirit. "The grace of God that bringeth salvation hath appeared to all men, teaching us that, denying ungodliness and worldly lusts, we should live soberly, righteously, and godly, in this present world; looking for that blessed hope, and the glorious appearing of the great God and our Saviour Jesus Christ." Titus ii.—11, 13. "For the kingdom of God is not meat and drink; but righteousness, and peace, and joy in the Holy Ghost; for he that in these things serveth Christ is acceptable to God, and approved of men." Rom. xiv.—17, 18. "Either make the tree good, and his fruit good; or else make the tree corrupt, and his fruit corrupt: for the tree is known by his fruit." Matt. xii.—33. This will make a bad tree good; and a good tree will bring forth good fruit." He shall sit as a refiner and purifier of silver; and he shall purify the sons of Levi, and purge them as gold and silver, that they may offer unto the Lord an offering in righteousness. Then shall the offering of Judah and Jerusalem be pleasant unto the Lord, as in the days of old, and as in former years." Mal. iii,—3, 4. A man may do many things, and may cast out devils: yet without this newness of service he will be a stink in God's nostrils: for without faith it is impossible to please him: and when that faith comes which is the gift of God, there will be a break-up or discharge and release from this schoolmaster the law, and this release is attended with love and joy unspeakable, and full of glory: accompanied by filial fear, which like a sentinal, keeps guard at the door of the heart, and will give the alarm at the movement of evil, and say, "how can I do this great wickedness, and sin against God?" Gen. xxxix. —9. " Behold, what manner of love the father hath bestowed upon us, that we should be called the sons of God." 1 John iii.---1. "Bless the Lord, O my soul, and forget not all his benefits; who forgiveth all thine iniquities; who healeth all thy diseases; who redeemeth thy life from destruction; who crowneth thee with loving kindness and tender mercies." Psa. ciii.----2, 4. There cannot be any thing so binding as love. The person in whom this love of God is not shed abroad, is under none other than the servants yoke; and all his service is in the oldness of the letter. But the Apostle declares that 'twas the love of Christ that constrained him; and he must be the basest character in existence, that can, without remorse, offend one that loves him with so great a love. The Apostle says, that he would do good; and the greatest good that we can do is to believe in him, to love him, to trust in him, and to give thanks unto him; and he has promised to work all our works in us.

But there is another class of law-men, that in word, hold or preach up the chastising or teaching by the father out of his law, to the awakening, alarming, and quickening of dead sinners; and but few of these hold the moral law to be a rule of life to a believer; yet they hold that the law after justification returns again and again, in its curse and terrors, and its killing feelings, for sin committed, or for backsliding. This I consider to be a great error, and one which ought to have been expunged by greater men than myself; but if no one else will shew this error, I will endeavour to do it; although I could have wished that some abler hand had done it.

For several years I was greatly tried and tossed, on this article of my faith. The Lord since he was pleased to cast the lot into my lap. Prov. xvi.---33. Which lot we are told causeth contentions to cease. Prov. xviii.---18. Hath often been pleased to shew me that the whole disposal thereof was of himself, and has hid himself that I could not find him, and when I called he gave me no answer, so that I have been ready to halt, my feet have well nigh slipped, and I have concluded that his mercy was clean gone; till my kness have been weak through fasting, I have been weary of my crying; my throat was dried; and mine eyes failed while I waited for my God. Psa. lxix.---3. At other times, the inbred corruptions of my flesh have betrayed me into the hand of the enemy; and I have been carried away captive; and I have been brought to see another law in my members, warring against the law of my mind, and bringing me into captivity to the law of sin which is in my members. And to say with Paul, O wretched man that I am! Who shall deliver me from the body of this death? Rom. vii.---23, 24. "If we say that we have no sin, we deceive ourselves, and the truth is not in us. If we confess our sins, he is faithful and just to forgive us our sins, and to cleanse us from all unrighteousness. If we say, that we have not sinned, we make him a liar, and his word is not in us." 1 John i.---8, 10. I have set down by the river of Babylon and wept when I remembered Zion, and have cried out, "Oh that I were as in months past, as in the days when God preserved me." Job. xxix.---2. I found that my corruptions were not destroyed, but instead of that, they struggled for the mastery. "Thou makest darkness, and it is night; wherein all the beasts of the forest do creep forth." Psa. civ.---20. The enemy would at these times insinuate that my God would visit me again in his wrath and anger, which temptation hath sunk me very low; for thought I, should this be the case, Alas! How shall I stand? As before I only, "escaped with the skin of my teeth." Job. xix.—20. And it is said that the righteous are but scarcely saved. 1 Pet. iv.—18. And to look back on those days in the fear of passing them again, has caused me to shudder, and to look closely after what men had to say; and as I found most of them on so important a point as this is, give an uncertain sound; sometimes saying, that it will not be so any more, at other times, almost in the same breath, saying, it may be and often is the case for a believer to pass through these things again; there could be no reliance placed on what they said. Well might the Psalmist say, who can know his errors? Certainly no one can till the Lord shews them to him.

These things are passed over lightly by those that are not in the storm; and others who have never passed from death to life, set it down for granted, that the law comes again and again; or contend for it only because some great man has wavered at times, and been on this weighty point as unstable as water, therefore he could not, in this, excel. Gen. xlix.—4. But I being in the storm, to me it was of the greatest moment, for between the two points I was tossed for five or six years, after the Lord gave me the spirit of adoption. Every time fresh guilt or darkness occurred, the enemy would represent to me that God would visit me again in his wrath; but in this I found the Devil to be a liar; for although God has often brought me to confess my foolishness and sins, and that I had procured all his chastisement to myself; and that in very faithfulness he had afflicted me. Psa. cxix.—75. "I will for this afflict the seed of David, but not for ever." 1 Kings xi.—39. Foolishness is bound in the heart of a child; and 'tis the rod of correction that must drive it out. Prov. xxii.—15. And my Lord has often made me sick by smiting me. Micah. vi.—13. Yet has he often deigned to comfort me after the days wherein he has shewn me trouble, and has washed my feet again, and restored the joy of salvation without any revelation of his anger or hot displeasure, but softly healed me by returning again, and shewing his mercy. "He will turn again, he will have compassion upon us: he will subdue our iniquities: and thou wilt cast all their sins into the depths of the sea." Micah. vii.----19. "Is Ephraim my dear son? Is he a pleasant child? For since I spake against him, I do earnestly remember him still; therefore my bowels are troubled for him; I will surely have mercy upon him, saith the Lord." Jer. xxxi.----20. At such unmerited kind dealings as these, has my heart often been made to melt; and they have endeared the Lord of life and glory to me; and at times, I have concluded, after such manifestations of his goodness and mercy, that he would never correct me again by the law. But Solomon says, that the legs of the lame are not equal, and so I found it to be.

I have often asked the Lord to indulge me in this particular, that I might be at a solid point in my Faith before that he would suffer me to handle it in public or private; and what the psalmist says, I found in this sense to be true, "By terrible things in righteousness wilt thou answer us, O God of our Salvation;" Psa. lxv. 5. for no sooner did the Lord decide this important point, and I began to advance it as the Lord's truth and my belief, than the blind bats fled as out of their holes, crying out, "This is as we would have it; Error: Error." When they had never seen a ray of the Sun of Righteousness arise on their souls, and all they could say, was only that I contradicted what such a man said. These blind could not see the distinction between a fallible man and a perfect man. This is an imperfect state; but when that which is perfect comes, then that that is imperfect shall be done away. And we read that the high priest went once a year into the holy place, and that not without blood, to offer for the errors of himself as well as for the people; and this we are told was a shadow of things to come; and shews to us that even priests are not perfect here. The Lord was pleased to send two portions of holy writ, with light and power into my heart, which decided the question in my mind, so that all doubt on this point with me is past. The first was this, "Behold I have taken out of thine hand the cup of trembling, even the dregs of the cup of my fury; thou shalt no more drink it again." Isa. li—22. The other, "In a little wrath I hid my face from thee for a moment; but with everlasting kindness will I have mercy on thee, saith the Lord thy Redeemer. For this is as the waters of Noah unto thee: for as I have sworn that the waters of Noah should no more go over the earth; so have I sworn that I would not be wroth with thee, nor rebuke thee." Isa. liv. 8,9.

Whatever affliction or darkness for the trial of my Faith the Lord has appointed for me, will certainly take place in his time. "For he performeth the thing that is appointed for me: and many such things are with him." Job xxiii. 14. But no more wrath is to be revealed, although "the flesh lusteth against the spirit, and the spirit against the flesh; and these are contrary the one to the other: so that ye cannot do the things that ye would. But if ye be led of the spirit, ye are not under the law." Gal. v.—17, 18. I do not fear any law that the French Government may make, because I know that I am not under its commands: so neither do I fear the law of Moses, as I am not under the law, but under Grace. "For God has not given us the spirit of fear; but of power, and of love, and of a sound mind." 2 Tim. i.—7. The Apostle cannot here mean filial fear: for God has promised to implant that in the heart; and that it shall abide for ever. Wherever this fear is not, all the profession will prove to be like the Gibeonites' wine-bottles, old, and rent, and bound up; and and their old shoes clouted upon their feet, and old garments upon them; and the bread of their provision, which was dry and mouldy. Jos. ix.—4, 5. But the Apostle's meaning is, that God will not send the law again that reveals from above and stirs from beneath, wrath; till the subject of it is brought into condemnation, for the Apostle declares that "There is therefore now no condemnation to them which are in Christ Jesus, who walk not after the flesh, but after the spirit." Rom. viii.—1.

Many have referred to Job to establish their favourite sentiment of the returning again of the law in its killing feelings. O what blindness hath befallen these men, that they cannot discern between the trial of faith and the curses of the law; 'tis evident by the claim that Job makes on the Lord, besides his referring to the day when the Lord delivered him. "Oh that I were as in months past, as in the days when God preserved me; when his candle shined upon my head, and when by his light I walked through darkness; as I was in the days of my youth, when the secret of God was upon my tabernacle;" Job xxix—2, 4. that the Lord cast him into a furnace to melt him, and shew him what dross still remained: and the afflictions he underwent, cast up plenty of the perverseness and fretfulness of the carnal mind; and in the whole body of sin, what impatience, what fretfulness, and what bitterness was manifested. Now hear what he says; he owns that he is in the furnace, and we see the dross swim at the top, "When he hath tried me, I shall come forth as gold." Job xxiii.--10. "For I know that my Redeemer liveth, and that he shall stand at the latter day upon the earth: and though after my skin worms destroy this body, yet in my flesh shall I see God: whom I shall see for myself, and mine eyes shall behold, and not another; though my reins be consumed within me." Job xix.--25, 27. "Also now, behold, my witness is in heaven, and my record is on high." Job xvi.--19. I would ask you this question: Could you, when labouring under the curse of the law, and the terrors of God, dare speak such language or claim with such boldness such high things? If you answer, "I could." I would not give one straw for all your faith. When the Lord first speaks to a sinner, the sinner draws back and "putteth his mouth in the dust; if so be there may be hope." Lam. iii.---29, He dares not speak nor adopt this language of Job.

But some may say, "suppose a man should fall foully, is he not to expect the same terror as he felt when the law was first sent home to him?" I answer, "No." Remember David, surely no man can fall fouler than he did; yet here being no unatoned guilt, as is felt under the curse of the law; there was no sinking in despair; but a deep sense of the evil, and an overcoming sense of God's goodness and forbearance. 2 Sam. xii.—13. Here is no fearful looking for of judgment, nor of fiery indignation, but fatherly correction; and what was the sentence? Not, " depart from me." But, " the sword shall never depart from thine house." that was, crosses, losses, and disappointments, with sorrow and afflictions. " Now no chastening for the present seemeth to be joyous, but grevious; nevertheless afterward it yielded the peaceable fruit of righteousness unto them which are exercised thereby." Heb. xii.—11. " I will visit their transgression with the rod, and their iniquity with stripes. Nevertheless my lovingkindness will I not utterly take from him, nor suffer my faithfulness to fail." Psa. lxxxix.—32, 33. This is the birthright of a son, that as nothing within and nothing without; no deservings in time past, present, or to come; was the cause, or can be the cause of our obtaining so high a privilege as to be a son of the most high; so nothing either within or without can be the cause of our forfeiting or being disinherited of the inheritance with the saints in light. " And of children, then heirs; heirs of God, and joint-heirs with Christ." Rom. viii.—17. " The servant abideth not in the house for ever; but the son abideth ever." John viii.—35. And our heavenly father knoweth how to make us sick in smiting us, (Mic. vi.—13.) without sending the law again; and this he does by withholding both light and comfort. "I went mourning without the sun." Job xxx.—28. "I will wait upon the Lord, that hideth his face from the house of Jacob, and I will look for him." Isa. viii.—17. Let the Lord hide himself, so as not to be found in the appointed means of his grace, nor in secret, nor in the inward peace, nor in meditation, nor in his providence; and let all be dark, and as to the comfortable enjoyment, thy evidences hid; and as to the life of God, or the graces of the spirit, all seem to be in a withering or lifeless state; which is his way of dealing with his children's faults; and this will bring them to consider, and say, "It was better with me in days that are past, than now." "Behold, I will hedge up thy way with thorns, and make a wall, that she shall not find her paths. And she shall follow after her lovers, but she shall not overtake them; and she shall seek them, but shall not find them; then shall she say, I will go and return to my first husband; for then it was better with me than now." Isa. ii.—6, 7. And this will produce many a secret confession, many a blushing face, many a groan, and many a cry. "Cast me not away, neither forsake me, but forgive and restore me." "He, being full [of] compassion, forgave their iniquity, and dest[roye]d them not; yea, many a time turned he [his a]nger away, and did not stir up all his w[rath]. For he remembered that they were but flesh: a wind that passeth away, and cometh not again." Psa. lxxviii.—38, 39. This will be their punishment, and a punishment that will make deep impression on a child without being driven by the terrors of the law into despair, which never will be thy case any more, "we are troubled on every side, yet not distressed: we are perplexed, but not in despair; persecuted but not forsaken; cast down, but not destroyed." 2 Cor. iv.—8, 9.

But some one may say, "I have known some hold this doctrine, whose moral life has been vile, and such as they ought to have been ashamed of." This I do not deny, (" for many walk, of whom I have told you often, and now tell you even weeping, that they are the enemies of the cross of Christ; whose end is destruction, whose God is their belly, and whose glory is in their shame, who mind earthly things.') Phil. iii—18, 19. And this may be the case with some; but if it be so, this grand truth has never been taught them by the holy spirit in the heart: if it had, there would have been a filial fear and a tender conscience implanted, " God maketh my heart soft." Job. xxiii.—16. And one of the greatest griefs of a child of God is that he cannot live in heart, lips, and thought, free from sin. "For the good that he would he does not, but the evil which he would not, that he do." Rom. vii.—19. and although he is blessed with this knowledge, that "I have blotted out, as a thick cloud, thy transgressions, and, as a cloud, thy sins: return unto me; for I have redeemed thee." Isa. xliv.—22. Sin will give sorrow to a child. But this truth may be holden in the head, or judgment, as well as any other truth. But if a man holds it only in his head or judgment, being destitute of the spirit of life imparted, he is but a thorn after all his profession; and we are not to expect grapes or figs from these, "by reason of whom the way of truth is evil spoken of." 2 Peter ii.--2. And of such as can live in sin without its being made to them a grief, bitterness, and cause of lamentation and woe. I will say as the Apostle saith, "Their judgment now of a long time lingereth not, and their damnation slumbereth not." 2 Peter ii.--2. And "Their damnation is just." Rom. iii.--8.

The Psalmist acknowledges with gratitude, that God was the author of his salvation. "Blessed be the Lord who daily loadeth us with his benefits, even the God of our salvation. He that is our God is the God of salvation; and unto God the Lord belong the issues from death." Psa. lxviii.---19, 20. And all that come through the strait of the new birth belong to God; and salvation signifies deliverance; one branch of salvation is, to be delivered from the penalty that is due to sin; another branch is, to be delivered from the guilt of sin by the application of the precious blood of Christ; and another branch of salvation is, to be delivered from the reigning power and dominion of sin; and another branch of salvation is, to be delivered from the love of sin according to the new nature that is imparted; and the next branch of salvation is, to be delivered from the in-being of sin: this last branch must be waited for until mortality is swallowed up of life; it was this last branch that the old patriarch Jacob waited for, when he said, " I have waited for thy salvation, O Lord." Gen. xlix.----18. " For the earnest expectation of the creature, waiteth for the manifestation of the sons of God." Rom. viii.----19. And then, "the inhabitant shall not say, I am sick." Isa. xxxiii.----24. This is what they are waiting for, and until this be their happy lot they will be subject to sickness; hope is an expectation of future good; and hope deferred maketh the heart sick; but O how sweet it is when accomplished, and then, and not till then, when sorrow and sighing will be completely done away. This the Apostle says, is the end of our faith, even the full salvation of our souls, and then our flesh will rest in hope until, " he shall change our vile body, that it may be fashioned like unto his glorious body, according to the working whereby he is able even to subdue all things unto himself." Phil. iii.—21.

One thing, before I close, I cannot omit giving my thoughts upon; and that is, the general practice of ministers in the ordinance of breaking of bread, or what is called the Sacrament of the Lord's Supper; not that I am going to speak slightingly or irreverently of that ordinance, the Lord forbid; I hold it in great esteem; but the manner in which it is administered, is what I have to observe upon; The minister invites, or presses, or admits persons to receive, and approves of their receiving the symbols of the death of the Lord Jesus Christ, who have never received his blood on their conscience to remove their guilt, nor the spirit's witness of their adoption, nor any sealing evidence of their redemption, nor any proclamation of their deliverance from imprisonment, nor any rising from the mystical death, having known nothing of the first resurrection; and never having eaten the flesh, nor drank the blood of the Lord Jesus Christ: and if they have not, hear what he says, " verily, verily, I say unto you, except ye eat the flesh of the son of man, and drink his blood, ye have no life in you." John vi.—53. How the minister can hand it knowingly to such as these, and how such as these can receive and partake of it, having no knowledge of their interest in it, I am astonished at. And how such can read the bare text that needs no comment." He took bread, and gave thanks, and brake it, and gave unto them, saying, this is my body which is given for you; this do in remembrance of me. Likewise also the cup after supper, saying, this cup is the New Testament in my blood, which is shed for you." Luke xxii.—19, 20. How dares such a character say, it was broken for him, or shed for him: when he has received no testimony of it by the spirit. "When he had given thanks, he brake it, and said, take, eat: this is my body, which is broken for you: this do in remembrance of me." 1 Cor. xi.—24.

The Apostle commands them to examine themselves before they partake, "let a man examine himself, and so let him eat of that bread, and drink of that cup. For he that eateth and drinketh unworthily, eateth and drinketh damnation to himself, not discerning the Lord's body." 1 Cor. xi.—28, 29. However bright a man's judgment may be in the doctrine or plan of redemption, that Christ suffered and bled in man's room and stead, and that this was for lost sinners; yet this is not discerning the Lord's body; for how know you, that you are one of them that he suffered so great an agony for, if he has not been revealed in you; but if he has, you have discerned by the spirit, that he has been roasted in the flame of the Father's wrath in your stead, and that his blood atoned and satisfied justice; and in such case justice does not stand to keep you from the tree of life any longer, neither is there any more wrath revealed.

The officiating minister hands the bread and wine, the outward symbols, with these words, " take, eat, this my body as broken for you ; take, drink, this cup, as my blood shed for you." Now, how dare he, to arrogate and take so great an authority on himself, when oftentimes condemned in his own conscience, and convinced that he is doing wrong, and knowing that he has no satisfactory testimony of the person he thus addresses being a worthy receiver, but quite the reverse. But surely this Scripture is fulfilled, " when thou sawest a thief, then thou consentedst with him, and hast been partaker with adulterers." Psa. L.—18. And the receiver takes it as the outward sign of, and in the character of one for whom, the body of Christ was broken, and his blood shed. But what says conscience? Does it never speak out, and condemn you for your presumption, at the time that in outward shew, you are commemorating the death of Christ, when you have never felt the blessed effect of it in your conscience to extirpate the sting of death? Surely such an one eateth and drinketh his own condemnation to a certainty, and however you may spurn and rebel against this warning, the day will come when you will remember that you were warned, although at present you may persist. " For he stretcheth out his hand against

God, and strengtheneth himself against the Almighty. He runneth upon him, even on his neck, upon the thick bosses of his bucklers." Job xv.—25, 26.

Some may say, that " those who partook of this Ordinance with our Lord, had no evidence of their interest in him." I pity your blindness: what did our Lord mean when he said, " rejoice not that the spirits are subject unto you ; but rather rejoice, because your names are written in Heaven." Luke x.—20. What heart can wish for more ; except only for the continuance of it in the life and sweet enjoyment thereof ? And again, " now ye are through the word which I have spoken unto you." John xv. —3. And again, " henceforth I call you not servants ; for the servant knoweth not what his Lord doeth : but I have called you friends ; for all things that I have heard of my father I have made known unto you." John xv.—15. " And I have declared unto them thy name, and will declare it ; that the love wherewith thou hast loved me may be in them, and I in them." John xvii.—26. Now the first manifestation of his name, is as a God of mercy, gracious, slow of anger, forgiving transgression and sin : and wherever this is the happy case, that man is born from on high. But if you mean that the Apostles had not received the Holy Ghost in all his light and illumination, to bring to their remembrance all things that they had heard and felt; I grant this to be true; for at that time the Scriptures were not opened up, nor were they till the day of pentecost, when they received the promise of the father. "He that believeth on me, as the scripture hath said, out of his belly shall flow rivers of living water; (but this spake he of the spirit, which they that believe on him should receive; for the Holy Ghost was not yet given; because that Jesus was not yet glorified.)" John vii.—38, 39. But who will dare to say that the Disciples were not believers, when John saith, that "his Disciples believed on him." John ii.—11.

But some to excuse themselves may say, "You are the wrong person to reprove us, for do not you live in the neglect of this ordinance in public?" In answer to which, I have some very substantial reasons why I have not hitherto celebrated it publicly; although I trust it will not always be so; and one reason why I have not been forward to do this, is, because I see that it is now with the professing world as it was in time past, for when the professing Church of Israel slid and fell from the true experimental life and power of the truth into the shadow and empty form of godliness, they kept up the empty shew; but the Lord despised that, and declared he was weary of it; see what he says in Isa. i. 11 to the 15. and in Amos v.—21. and Luke xiii. 25, 27. For without faith it is impossible to please him, and this faith must be wrought by

Divinity itself; not a human or natural faith so common in our day; for we are told that he that is in the flesh cannot please God; and where there has not been a planting in the likeness of Christ's death, and rising by the self-same power that brought him up from the dead, there is nothing but flesh.

Some of my readers may wish to know whether I had any thing particular in my view, in the naming of my children. I had: and for your information, I will, in as short a manner as possible, shew you. To my first-born I gave the name of "Reuben," which signifies, Who sees the Son, or vision of the Son. And Paul says, "It pleased God to reveal his dear Son in me the Hope of Glory." And my desire is, if it be consistent with his will, that his name may be fully verified by the same vision or revelation. "Let Reuben live, and not die; and let not his men be few. Deut. xxxviii.—6. But the cause of his name on my part sprang from this: I had long been in great distress on account of the loss of my immortal soul; and it appeared that the Lord had appointed me to wrath, as nothing but wrath was revealed, and I often felt what the prophet said, "they shall pass through it, hardly bestead and hungry: and it shall come to pass, that when they shall be hungry, they shall fret themselves, and curse their king and their God, and look upward. And they shall look unto the earth; and behold trouble and darkness, dimness of anguish; and they shall be driven to darkness." Isa. viii.—21, 22. And this I concluded would be my end. But the Lord's thoughts were not as my thoughts; for instead of ending in so awful a state as this, the Lord in love and mercy appeared, and delivered my soul from death and my eyes from tears. On this account I named him as I did, so that when I looked on him it might put me in remembrance of the cause. "She called his name Reuben: for she said, surely the Lord hath looked upon my affliction;" Gen. xxix.—33. and this was the declaration of Jacob, "Reuben, thou art my first born, my might, and the beginning of my strength, the excellency of dignity, and the excellency of power" Gen. xlix.—3.

The next of my children was a daughter; to her I gave the name of Martha, which signifies, becoming bitter, and caring for many things. Luke x.—40, 41. At the time of her birth, the Nation was groaning under the oppression of the Forestaller and Monopoliser, until flour arrived to the enormous price of three shillings and four-pence per gallon, and in many places, four shillings, "and they made their lives bitter with hard bondage." Exod. i.—14. "Surely Oppression maketh a wise man mad." Eccles. vii.—7. "He that withholdeth corn, the people shall curse him: but blessing shall be upon the head of him that selleth it." Prov. xi. 26. This being an artificial famine, it made me oftentimes fret, and at times bitter; as my income was very small; and the fear that I should not be able to pay all my debts would often grieve me, as I can say with truth, that it always was a reigning desire of my heart to pay every one their own; and after all my fears I have been enabled so to do. But at that time how many carping cares I had, and how incumbered indeed, I felt myself to be, about the things that perish; to the great grief of the new man. I hope my readers may never see such days as these were, and to this day when I look on my daughter, it often brings afresh to my remembrance, the days that are past, and moreover, I have missed my mark, if she does not find on her account that I named her rightly. But 'tis said that our Lord loved Martha as well as Mary; and O, if it be the Lord's will, may she share in so great a love!

The next of my offspring, was a son; I named him Benjamin. Gen. xxxv. 17, 18. I had for several months previous to the birth of this son laboured under a very heavy trial, and was greatly cast down, and often doubted whether the Lord would appear for me again, and at times made many a hasty conclusion; and when my spirits were depressed, I concluded that I would name the child, if a son, Benoni, the son of my sorrow: but the Lord was pleased to surprise me, by delivering me out of this sore temptation, just before his birth: now, said I, he shall be called

Benjamin, the son of my right-hand, and to this day when I look on him, it brings fresh to my mind the sorrows that befel me in that day, and the deliverance that the Lord wrought for me. And, if it be the Lord's will, may he share in the blessing pronounced on his namesake. And of Benjamin he said, "The beloved of the Lord shall dwell in safety by him; and the Lord shall cover him all the day long, and he shall dwell between his shoulders." Deut, xxxiii.—12.

The next son that was born I named Abraham, which signifies, an high father, or the father of elevation or of great multitude. How this may prove to be true with my son I know not, but, if it be the Lord's will, he is able, seeing all things are possible with him; therefore I desire to leave this. But the cause of his receiving his name was this: a great change in providence about to take place, whereon depended much future good or adversity as to the things of this life; and as this drew near, the cloud gathered thicker and darker; but the crisis came, and such a crisis as I never shall forget. The Lord bid Abraham to go out, but Abraham knew not whither he was going. Heb. xi.---8. Gen. xii.---1. The Lord led his servant forth in an unknown way to bring him to the decreed place, safe and sure, although it was hid at the time from his sight, and so it was from mine. If it be the Lord's will, may my son be led by the same unerring hand through life, and be brought to the city whose builder and maker is God. This son is a memorial to us.

And to my last son I gave the name of Joseph, which signifies increase or addition. "And of Joseph he said, blessed of the Lord be his land, for the precious things of heaven, for the dew, and for the deep that coucheth beneath." Deut. xxxiii.--13. "Joseph is a fruitful bough even a fruitful bough by a well; whose branches run over the wall: the archers have sorely grieved him, and shot at him, and hated him: but his bow abode in strength, and the arms of his hands were made strong by the hands of the mighty God of Jacob; (from thence is the shepherd, the stone of Israel:") Gen. xlix. 22, 24. Every branch that abideth in Christ bringeth forth fruit, and to be in him as a branch or a bough signifies in the first place, being so by predestination, or being appointed and chosen of God the Father before the world was made. "According as he hath chosen us in him before the foundation of the world, that we should be holy and without blame before him in love: having predestinated us unto the adoption of children by Jesus Christ to himself, according to the good pleasure of his will." Eph. i.--4, 5. And in time to be cut out of the wild olive tree, and then to be ingrafted, or to enter by the manifestation of the spirit, into him, as a graft is conveyed into the stock. "I am the vine, ye are the branches," and "from me is your fruit found." This fruit is love, faith, hope, joy, long-suffering, and so forth. "Thou, which hast shewed me great and sore troubles, shalt quicken me again, and shalt bring me up again from the depths of the earth. Thou shalt increase my greatness, and comfort me on every side." Psa. lxxi.—20, 21. May God of his great mercy bless his land, for the precious things of heaven, for the dew, and for the deep that coucheth beneath; and may the God of his father help him when he is brought into trouble. But the cause of this name being given to him was this, when this son was born there was a great opposition and persecution against me, because, in my preaching, I insisted on the necessity of the death of a sinner being known and felt under the law, and of a free pardon being proclaimed through the blood of Christ. Ephes. i.—7. At this time old friends forsook me, and turned to be my sworn enemies, and were crying out he hath a devil and is mad, and as they cried against the brethren " These that have turned the world upside down are come hither also." Acts xvii. 6. It is said that Joseph was a fruitful bough by a well; whose branches run over the wall: and that the archers shot at him, and hated him. If this has not been the exact case between my opposers and me I hope you will shew it. They opposed me in my ministry; and did me all the mischief they could, both in my name and in my little trade; still I was enabled to stand, and cry aloud, and shew unto Jacob his transgression, and to Israel his sin; and to witness both to small and great, that nothing short of blood applied could remove guilt; and they kept shooting, and predicting of my fall, and shot bitter words at the upright in heart. Nevertheless my bow abode in great strength, because the arms of my hands were made strong by the mighty God of Israel. Therefore I called his name Joseph, and may the Lord give him favour in the eyes of the Egyptians.

I have three desires in my heart, which I hope may be granted me in this life, if it be consistent with the will of the Lord. The first is, that I may not consider my own life, "neither count it dear unto myself, so that I might finish my course with joy, and the ministry, which I have received of the Lord Jesus, to testify the Gospel of the Grace of God." Acts xx. —24. But that the truth and honour of my Lord and Master, may outweigh all my own honour and all the good in this life; that I may be steadfast, unmovable, always abounding in work of the Lord; and be faithful unto and he will give me a crown of life. nd is, that the Lord would be pleased appoint and away, and the whirlwind shall scatter them: and that he shall rejoice in the Lord, and glory in the Holy One of Israel. Isa. xli.—15, 16. But also cause him to be made manifest before I depart, that I may say as Jacob did, "It is enough." Gen. xlv.—28. And then yield up my office into the hands of a faithful successor, and my spirit into the hands of the Lord of Life and Glory.—And the third is, that my present Sovereign Lord, the King, may be spared to live and reign in peace, as long as I live to be a Subject of this Realm.

And I can truly say, that I forgive all liars against me, and all my slanderers, and all evil speakers and surmisers; for although they meant the whole for evil, the Lord has caused it to work for good, as he meant it should: and may the Lord give them repentance to life. Matt. vi.—15.

Now unto the King eternal, immortal, invisible, the only wise God, be honour and glory for ever and ever. Amen and Amen.

"God moves in a mysterious way,
His wonders to perform;
He plants his footsteps in the sea,
the storm.

Ye fearful saints fresh courage take,
   The clouds ye so much dread
Are big with mercy, and shall break
   In blessings on your head.

Judge not the Lord by feeble sense,
   But trust him for his grace;
Behind a frowning providence,
   He hides a smiling face.

His purposes will ripen fast,
   Unfolding ev'ry hour;
The bud may have a bitter taste,
   But sweet will be the flow'r.

Blind unbelief is sure to err,
   And scan his work in vain;
God is his own interpreter,
   And he will make it plain."

Lower, Printer, Bookseller & Stationer, High-street, Lewes.

www.ingramcontent.com/pod-product-compliance
Lightning Source LLC
Chambersburg PA
CBHW080437110426
42743CB00016B/3194